The Directory of Publishers in Religion

SCHOLARS PRESS
HANDBOOK SERIES

The Directory of Publishers in Religion

compiled by
Mike Farry

The Directory of Publishers in Religion

compiled by
Mike Farry

Scholars Press
Atlanta, Georgia

The Directory of Publishers in Religion

compiled by
Mike Farry

Copyright ©1997
Scholars Press

Library of Congress Cataloging in Publication Data
The directory of publishers in religion / compiled by Mike Farry.
      p.   cm. — (Scholars Press handbook series ; 10)
      Includes indexes.
      ISBN 0-7885-0410-X (pbk. : alk. paper)
      1. Religious literature—Publishing—United States—Directories.
2. Religious literature—Authorship—Directories.   I. Farry, Mike.
II. Series.
Z479.D57   1997
070.5'025'73—dc21   97-40271
                               CIP

Printed in the United States of America
on acid-free paper

Contents

Preface

This directory launches the first comprehensive, regularly updated listing of publishers in the field of religion. Embracing all facets of religious thought and life, the *Directory* contains publishers representing most of the world's major faith traditions, many new religions, as well as the study of religion. While a special effort has been made to list publishers specializing in religious scholarship, the companies listed here serve the full continuum of religious publishing for secular, denominational, and non-denominational audiences of all sizes. Thus, within these pages you will find publishers seeking a diverse range of new works, from guides for the daily life of believers to inspirational children's fiction, from religious education materials to examinations of the cultural and political role of religion, from resources for fostering interfaith dialogue to new reference works, and beyond. In all these instances, the *Directory* is designed primarily for the prospective author, focusing its attention on each publisher's editorial mission, acquisitions needs and submission guidelines.

Compilation

The participants in this directory responded to a survey of publishers in the United States that devote a significant portion of their book publishing program to religion-related topics. Potential participants were identified either by the Library of Congress subject headings of their titles or from their self-descriptions in directories of the publishing trade. No distinction of creed, number of titles, or other criterion governed the selection of publishers solicited for inclusion. In keeping with the *Directory's* emphasis on editorial objectives and policies, the survey questionnaire was, whenever possible, completed by a member of each participant's acquisitions staff. Except for minor changes arising from formatting requirements, the *Directory's* contents were composed entirely by the participants themselves.

How to Use this Directory

Each entry in the *Directory's* alphabetical listing contains some or all of the following information (note that some publishers have listed each of their imprints in individual entries):

Entry Number: Publishers are indexed by this number, indicating their numerical position in the *Directory's* alphabetical listing. This is also the number referenced in the *Directory's* running headers (page numbers are found on the bottom of each page).

Company Name: The full name of the publisher or imprint.

Subsidiary/Division of: The publisher's parent organization.

Imprint of: If applicable, the full name of the publisher of this imprint.

Main Address: The address of the company's headquarters; unless otherwise indicated, manuscript submissions should be sent here.

Additional Address(es): Any other addresses (street, warehouse, separate editorial offices, etc.) the publisher has identified; a description precedes each additional address.

Phone: The telephone number of the company's headquarters is listed first; when included, additional phone numbers (for orders, etc.) will follow with accompanying parenthetical descriptions.

Fax: As with the phone numbers, the first number listed usually belongs to the company's main offices, followed by any additional fax numbers and their relevant descriptions.

E-mail: The electronic mail address for Internet correspondence with the company.

WWW Homepage: The URL of the publisher's World Wide Web site; all WWW addresses in this directory should be preceded by "http://" when directing your browser.

Corporate Staff: In the instance a publisher has so chosen, a list of senior personnel follows below the address information. Note that acquisitions staff are listed separately (see *Send Submissions to* below).

Faith/Denominational/Cultural Focus: If the publisher concentrates on a specific faith/denominational tradition or on the religions of particular cultures, that emphasis is indicated here. In most cases, publishers listing such a focus will not consider any manuscripts for publication that do not address the appropriate tradition (unless otherwise indicated in the *Description of Editorial Program* below). An index of publishers by faith/denominational/cultural focus follows the alphabetical listing of entries (see the section of this Preface on **Indexing**).

Subject Areas: This field contains a list of religion-related subject areas appropriate to the publisher's editorial program. These broad categories are intended for general indexing purposes (see **Indexing** section for more information on the categories); for the precise details of the publisher's area of interest, consult the *Description of Editorial Program* section. Note also that any subject interest identified by a publisher should always be cross-referenced with its *Faith/Denominational/Cultural Focus*; for instance, a Roman Catholic publisher indicating an interest in the "History of Religion" would generally accept only those historical studies devoted to the Catholic tradition.

Types of Publications: The formats (trade books, electronic media, etc.), audiences (children, adults, students, etc.) and genres (reference, fiction, monographs, etc.) in and for which the company regularly publishes religion-related texts. As with the *Subject Areas* above, these categories are inexact, intended to provide a general index (see the **Indexing** section below) and are always qualified by the *Faith/Denominational/Cultural Focus* appropriate to the publisher.

Description of Editorial Program: Generally, the "Types of Publications" field is followed by a detailed explanation of the mission and objectives sustaining the publisher's editorial program. In addition to providing specifics regarding the *Faith/ Denominational/Cultural Focus, Subject Areas*, and *Types of Publications* listed above, this section may contain information about the publisher's history, the values that shape its acquisitions policies, and previously published authors and titles.

Acquisitions Focus for 1998-9: The specific kinds of manuscripts sought by editorial staff during the period covered by this directory.

Titles in Print/New in 1997/ISBN Prefix(es): These figures pertain to the publisher's religion-related titles.

Percentage of Titles Subsidized by Authors: If the company engages in author-subsidized publishing, this is the approximate percentage of previously-published titles which required author funding.

Recent/Upcoming Titles: Up to three religion-related titles new in 1997 or forthcoming in 1998.

How to Obtain Manuscript Guidelines: This field indicates that the publisher's manuscript guidelines can be obtained in one of three ways: 1) free on request, 2) with a self-addressed, stamped 1st class business envelope (if a larger envelope or additional postage is required, it will be indicated) or 3) in rare cases, for a fee. Should the company not publish rules for manuscript submissions, the field reads "No manuscript guidelines available."

Preferred Form of Initial Contact: This is the procedure prospective authors should follow when submitting material for the publisher's consideration. Publishers usually request one of the following:

1) Short written query: a brief letter describing the manuscript's subject, length, intended audience, distinguishing qualities, pervious books by the same author, similar titles, and other pertinent information.

2) Proposal package: some combination of a cover letter, chapter outline, sample chapters, SASE, author biography, and other material, as indicated.

Alternately, this section will read "Agented submissions only" in the event the publisher restricts its consideration to authors with literary agents, or "No unsolicited submissions accepted" if the publisher will not consider manuscripts it has not previously requested. Note that prospective authors should consult the publisher's manuscript guidelines, when available, before submitting any material (see previous section).

Send Submissions to— This section lists the names and titles of the publisher's religion acquisitions staff to whom queries or proposals should be directed. If multiple editors are listed, each name is often preceded by the subject areas or types of publications appropriate for his or her consideration.

Acquisitions Address: If the publisher's acquisitions offices differ from its headquarters, the acquisitions address is listed here. Otherwise, submit manuscripts to the appropriate staff at the main address.

Limitations/Restrictions: Any further qualifications governing manuscript submissions.

Indexing

As noted above, publisher entries in the alphabetical listing are referenced by entry number in three indexes at the end of this volume.

1. The *Faith/Denominational/Cultural Focus Index* contains a listing of publishers that exclusively emphasize specific faith traditions, denominational communities, or cultures. Non-sectarian or secular

publishers are not referenced in this index; it is generally more effective to consult the *Subject Area Index* for such publishers.

2. The *Subject Area Index* consists of six sections: 1) Religious Life/Practice, 2) Religious Thought/Theology, 3) Religious Studies, 4) Religion and Society, 5) Sacred Literature, and 6) Religious Education. A general outline of and selected topics found in each section follows:

2.1 *Religious Life/Practice* encompasses discussion and guidance of the daily life and practice of religious individuals, professionals, and communities. Topics include Liturgy/Ritual, Prayer/Meditation, Vocational/Pastoral Guidance, Preaching/Homiletics, Missions, Spiritual Life/Personal Religion, Religion and the Family, Religion and Health, and Religious Biography.

2.2 *Religious Thought/Theology* concerns the examination of issues of doctrine, metaphysics, and related, from within a specific faith tradition or religious context. Topics include: Ethics, Doctrinal Theology & Dogma, Process Theology, Pastoral Theology, Systematic Theology, Natural Theology, Theological Education (Methodology), and Pluralistic and Ecumenical Theology.

2.3 *Religious Studies* corresponds roughly to the subjects addressed by the academic discipline of religious studies. Topics include: Comparative Religions, History of Religion(s), Mythology, Folklore, Sacred Languages, Interdisciplinary Studies (Philosophy of Religion, Anthropology of Religion, Ethnic Studies and Religion, etc.), and Methodologies of Study and Teaching.

2.4 The *Religion and Society* section addresses the investigation and discussion of the interaction between religious communities, doctrines, and values and contemporary social, political, legal, and cultural issues. Topics include: Religion in Popular Culture/Media, Religion and Law, Religion and Public Policy.

2.5 *Sacred Literature* includes topics related to the literature of the world's major faith traditions, including Commentary & Hermeneutics, Philology & Linguistics, Cultural & Historical Contexts, and Translations. In addition to the general category "Sacred Literature," this section also contains separate listings for specific textual traditions (Biblical, Talmudic, etc.).

2.6 *Religious Education* publications for use in the formal religious education of all ages. Topics include: Theory and Methodology, Public Policy/Legal Issues, and Elementary- through Adult-level classroom materials.

These classifications are derived from those established by the Library of Congress, other directories of the publishing trade, and other surveys of the field of religion. As such, they contain unavoidable imprecision and redundancy; for more detailed information, consult each publisher's entry.

3. The *Types of Publications Index* lists publishers by the audiences, formats, and genres appropriate to their editorial programs. These include Fiction, Poetry, Scholarly Monographs, Audio-Visual, Electronic Publications, References of various types, and more.

Future Editions

We currently plan to update the *Directory* every two years, with the next edition expanded to incorporate both international publishers and those U.S. organizations not included in this volume. While we have endeavored to achieve an exhaustive scope in the first edition, it inevitably suffers errors and omissions. We would appreciate hearing either of such errors or from publishers who would like to receive the next survey. Contact us by writing to: The Directory of Publishers in Religion, Scholars Press, PO Box 15399, Atlanta, GA 30333-0399.

Acknowledgments

This project owes its existence to generous support of the Lilly Endowment, Inc., which has long made essential contributions to the success of the Scholars Press consortium. In addition, our thanks are due to all the editors and personnel at the participating publishers who devoted their time, counsel, and expertise to the compilation of this *Directory*.

Alphabetical Listing of Publishers

1 Abingdon Press

Subsidiary/division of The United Methodist Publishing House
PO Box 801, Nashville, TN 37202-0801
Academic Editorial Office: 2495 Lawrenceville Hwy, Decatur, GA 30033
Phone: 615-749-6403, 404-636-6001 (academic editorial)
Fax: 615-749-6512, 404-636-5894 (academic editorial)
WWW homepage: www.abingdon.org
Subject areas: Liturgy and Ritual, Prayer & Meditation, Vocational/Pastoral Guidance, Preaching & Homiletics, Missions, Spiritual Life/Personal Religion, Religion and the Family, Ethics, Doctrinal Theology & Dogma, Process Theology, Systematic Theology, Pastoral Theology, Theological Education (methodology), Pluralistic/Ecumenical Theology, Religion in Popular Culture/Media, Religion and Public Policy, Biblical Literature — Commentary & Hermeneutics, Biblical Literature — Philology & Linguistics, Biblical Literature — Cultural & Historical Contexts, Religious Education — Theory and Methodology
Types of publications: Classroom Instructional Materials, Electronic Publications (CD-ROM), Music, Essay/Lecture Collections, Reprints, Devotional Guides, Liturgical Materials, General Interest Nonfiction — Adult, General Interest Nonfiction — Juvenile, Scholarly Monographs, General Reference, Language Reference, Academic Reference
Abingdon Press publishes religious books which advance knowledge and facilitate praxis within the academic community (colleges, universities, and seminaries), with an emphasis on the United Methodist denominational market, in the areas of Biblical studies, church history, theology and philosophy, ethics and social issues, pastoral care and counseling, spirituality, liturgy and worship, practical theology, congregational ministries, homiletics, Christian education, and Wesleyan and Methodist studies. Within these subject areas, Abingdon Press publishes both multi-volume and single-volume reference works; monographs that provide a forum for original, specialized scholarly research; general academic books that address topics and issues of contemporary significance and relevance

1

in the scholarly world; and textbooks that summarize special knowledge for students in classroom studies. The Kingswood Books and United Methodist Studies Publications programs provide special resources for Methodist and Wesleyan studies.

Acquisitions focus for 1998-9: Biblical studies, church history, practical theology, pastoral care and counseling, spirituality.

In print: 500 titles.   1997: 50 titles.   ISBN Prefix(es): 0-687

Recent/Forthcoming Titles: Miroslav Volf, *Exclusion and Embrace: A Theological Exploration of Identity, Otherness, and Reconciliation*; J. Louis Martyn, *Theological Issues in the Letters of Paul*; Mark G. Toulouse & James O. Duke (eds.), *Makers of Christian Theology in America*

Manuscript guidelines free upon request

Preferred form of initial contact: Short written query or formal proposal following MS guidelines (request first)

Send submissions to—

Books for academic audience: Ulrike Guthrie, Editor, Academic Books (at Atlanta office)

Books for clergy & religious professionals: Dr. Robert A. Ratcliff, Senior Editor, Professional Books (at Nashville office)

Books for general readers: Mary Catherine Dean, Senior Editor, General Interest Books (at Nashville office)

2 Academic International Press

PO Box 1111, Gulf Breeze, FL 32562-1111

Fax: 904-932-5479

E-mail: bevon@gulf.net

WWW homepage: www.pcola.net/~bevon

Types of publications: Academic Reference (Encyclopedias)

Academic International Press publishes *The Modern Encyclopedia of Religion in Russia and the Soviet Union*, a multi-volume work covering all aspects of religion practiced in Russia, the Soviet Union, and post-Soviet states from ancient times to the present, and *Religious Documents Annual*, an annual collection of primary source documents recounting the developments in religion in the U.S. and Canada.

In print: 2 titles.

ISBN Prefix(es): 0-87569

No manuscript guidelines available

No unsolicited submissions accepted

3 Accent Publications
Subsidiary/division of Cook Communications Ministry
PO Box 36640, Colorado Springs, CO 80936
Street Address: 4050 Lee Vance View, Colorado Springs, CO 80918
Faith/denominational/cultural focus: Christian
Subject areas: Christian Ed. ministry of local church
In print: 60 titles.
ISBN Prefix(es): 0-89636
Send #10 SASE for manuscript guidelines
Preferred form of initial contact: Short written query with SASE.
Send submissions to—
   Mary Nelson

4 ACTA Publications
4848 N Clark St, Chicago, IL 60640
Phone: 773-271-1030
Fax: 773-271-7399
E-mail: acta@one.org
Co-Publisher: Thomas R. Artz
Co-Publisher: Gregory F. Pierce
Faith/denominational/cultural focus: Roman Catholic, Protestant
Subject areas: Liturgy and Ritual, Prayer & Meditation, Spiritual Life/Personal Religion, Religion and the Family, Pastoral Theology, Religion and Art, Religious Education — Adult
Types of publications: Books-on-Tape, Audio-Visual, Music, Devotional Guides, General Interest Nonfiction — Adult
Assisting Christians To Act Publications publishes books, and video and audio tape programs for adults in Catholic and mainline Protestant denominations. Topics include adult study, basic Church teachings, spirituality, marriage preparation, and family enrichment.
Acquisitions focus for 1998-9: Adult lay spirituality, faith and workplace, Catholic doctrinal matters, and marriage preparation and enrichment.
In print: 125 titles.   1997: 15 titles.
ISBN Prefix(es): 0-87946; 0-915388; 0-914070
Send #10 SASE for manuscript guidelines
Preferred form of initial contact: Proposal package containing query, SASE, outline, and 1 sample chapter.
Send submissions to—
   Gregory F. Augustine Pierce, Co-Publisher

5   ACU Press

Subsidiary/division of Abilene Christian University
ACU Box 29138, Abilene, TX 79699
Phone: 915-674-2720
Fax: 915-674-6471
Managing Director: Thom Lemmons
Faith/denominational/cultural focus: Church of Christ
Subject areas: Preaching & Homiletics, Missions, Spiritual Life/ Personal Religion, Religion and the Family, Doctrinal Theology & Dogma, History of Religion(s), Religion and Literature, Biblical Literature — Commentary & Hermeneutics
Types of publications: Devotional Guides, General Reference, Bible Study — Adult
Primary mission is to publish materials useful for personal and class study and material of doctrinal or historical interest to the Church of Christ fellowship. Secondary mission is to publish personal and class study and devotional material appropriate for an evangelical Christian audience.
In print: 120 titles.   1997: 5 titles.
ISBN Prefix(es): 0-89112, 0-915547
Recent/Forthcoming Titles: *Equipped for Change: Studies in the Pastoral Epistles; The Main Thing: A New Look at Ecclesiastics; Shadow and Light: Literature and the Life of Faith*
No manuscript guidelines available
Preferred form of initial contact: Short written query
Send submissions to—
     Thom Lemmons, Managing Director

6   Alba House

2187 Victory Blvd, Staten Island, NY 10314
Phone: 718-761-0047
Fax: 718-761-0057
Editor: Edmund C. Lane
Assoc. Editor: Frank Sadowski
Faith/denominational/cultural focus: Roman Catholic, Christian
Subject areas: Prayer & Meditation, Preaching & Homiletics, Religious Biography, Ethics, Doctrinal Theology & Dogma, Systematic Theology, Pastoral Theology, Biblical Literature — Commentary & Hermeneutics

Types of publications: General Interest Nonfiction — Adult
In print: 250 titles.   1997: 24 titles.
ISBN Prefix(es): 0-8189
Manuscript guidelines free upon request
Preferred form of initial contact: Proposal package containing SASE
  and full manuscript.

7   The Alban Institute, Inc

7315 Wisconsin Ave, Suite 1250W, Bethesda, MD 20814
Phone: 301-718-4407
Fax: 301-718-1958, 301-718-1966 (orders)
President: James P. Wind
Exec. Vice President: Leslie L. Buhler
Subject areas: Vocational/Pastoral Guidance, Spiritual Life/Personal
  Religion, Religion and Music, Religion and Cultural/Ethnic Studies,
  Religion and Gender Studies, Sociology of Religion, Religion in
  Popular Culture/Media, Religion and Public Policy, Religious
  Education — Seminary, Religious Education — Adult
Types of publications: Self-Help, Scholarly Monographs, Dissertations,
  General Reference, Academic Reference
The Alban Institute works to encourage congregations to be vigorous
  and faithful so that they may equip the people of God to minister
  within their faith communities and in the world. To assist those who
  lead or care for congregations, the Institute gathers, generates, and
  shares practical knowledge across denominational lines through
  publications and other means. The Alban Institute engages in
  research on congregational faith and life at the local level across
  denominational lines. We publish research-based resources.
Acquisitions focus for 1998-9: The Alban Institute is interested in
  publishing a series of books or other resources on the topic "Money,
  Lifestyle, and Faith." One goal of the series is to overcome the
  compartmentalization of faith and money-matters. Other focuses
  include the church's service as facilitator of public discourse; interim
  ministry; addressing Biblical illiteracy and spiritual development in
  the congregation.
In print: 100+ titles.   1997: 10 titles.
Recent/Forthcoming Titles: *Plain Talk about Churches and Money; A
  Safe Place to Talk about Homosexuality; Financial Meltdown in the
  Mainline*

5

Send SASE w/2 oz. 1st class postage for MS guidelines
Preferred form of initial contact: Proposal package containing outline
  and sample chapter (call or write to us for our list of questions first).
Send submissions to—
  Linda-Marie Delloff, Director of Publishing

8 Alleluia Press

672 Franklin Turnpike, Allendale, NJ 07401
Owner/CEO: Dr. José M. de Vinck
Faith/denominational/cultural focus: Eastern Orthodox
Subject areas: Liturgy and Ritual, Prayer & Meditation, Spiritual
  Life/Personal Religion, Ethics, Pluralistic/Ecumenical Theology,
  Comparative Religions, History of Religion(s), Philosophy of
  Religion, Biblical Literature — Translations
Types of publications: Liturgical Materials, Fiction — Adult, Poetry
Books of Oriental Rites interest: the philosophical, theological, and
  literary works of Dr. José M. de Vinck.
In print: 28 titles.
 10% of titles author-subsidized
ISBN Prefix(es): 0-911726
Recent/Forthcoming Titles: *Faith in the New Age*
No manuscript guidelines available
No unsolicited submissions accepted

9 American Bio Center

Subsidiary/division of American Biographical Center
Rte 658, North River Shore, North, VA 23128
Phone: 804-725-2234
Fax: 804-725-2234
E-mail: hone@inna.net
WWW homepage: www.inna.net/biocenter
Vice President: Lou Hone
Faith/denominational/cultural focus: New Age (Global)
Subject areas: Religion and Health, Comparative Religions, Philosophy
  of Religion, Religion in Popular Culture/Media
Types of publications: General Interest Nonfiction — Adult

America Bio Center publishes works related to global, universal, New Age.

In print: 2 titles. 1997: 1 title.

Send $50 for manuscript guidelines

Preferred form of initial contact: Proposal package containing SASE and entire manuscript. Agented submissions only.

Send submissions to—

Harry Hone, President

10   American Catholic Press

16565 South State Street, South Holland, IL 60473

Phone: 708-331-5485

Fax: 708-331-5484

Executive Director: Rev. Michael Gilligan, Ph.D.

Manager/Vice President: Joan Termini

Information Systems Manager/Corporate Secretary: Wendy Loggins

Faith/denominational/cultural focus: Roman Catholic

Subject areas: Liturgy and Ritual, Prayer & Meditation, Doctrinal Theology & Dogma, Religion and Music

Types of publications: Music, Illustrated Books, Liturgical Materials

We publish periodicals, books, and recordings either for use directly in the liturgy, for preparation of the liturgy, or for understanding of the liturgy. For use in the liturgy, we publish musical settings of Psalms and hymns, hymnals, the *Leaflet Missal*, choral octavos, and instrumental arrangements. For preparation of the liturgy, we publish *Parish Liturgy* (a quarterly), as well as various books and tapes. For understanding the liturgy, we publish more extensive books and other materials.

In print: 25 titles.   1997: 2 titles.

ISBN Prefix(es): 0-915866

Recent/Forthcoming Titles: *Singing the Psalms*; *Guide for the Parish Musician*; *Sing to the Lord*

No manuscript guidelines available

No unsolicited submissions accepted

Send submissions to—

Michael Gilligan, Editorial Director

Limitations/Restrictions: No poetry or material of a general religious nature; our interest is strictly in liturgy, liturgical theology, history of liturgy, and liturgical music.

11   Andrews University Press

213 Information Services Bldg, Berrien Springs, MI 49103

Phone: 616-471-6915, 800-467-6369 (Visa/MC orders), 616-471-6134 (other orders)

Fax: 616-471-6224

E-mail: aupress@andrews.edu

Director: Carol Loree

Faith/denominational/cultural focus: Seventh-Day Adventist

Subject areas: Religious Biography, Doctrinal Theology & Dogma, History of Religion(s), Religion and Archaeology, Religious Education — Theory and Methodology, Religious Education — Public policy/Legal Issues

Types of publications: Essay/Lecture Collections, Dissertations, Language Reference

Andrews University Press primarily publishes the scholarly studies and dissertations of faculty and students at SDA Theological Seminary.

Acquisitions focus for 1998-9: Accepting no manuscripts

ISBN Prefix(es): 1-943872; 0-8467-0071

Recent/Forthcoming Titles: *Faith, Reason, and Earth History: A Paradigm of Earth and Biological Origins by Intelligent Design*

Manuscript guidelines free upon request

Preferred form of initial contact: Proposal package containing outline and 2 sample chapters.

12   Ashgate Publishing Company

Subsidiary/division of Ashgate Publishing Co, Ltd

Old Post Road, Brookfield, VT 05036

Phone: 802-276-3162, 800-535-9544 (Toll free)

Fax: 802-276-3651, 802-276-3837 (cust. svc./orders)

E-mail: info@ashgate.com

WWW homepage: www.ashgate.com

Publisher: John Smalley

International Marketing Manager: Barbara J. Church

Faith/denominational/cultural focus: Christian, Islamic, Judaism

Subject areas: Comparative Religions, History of Religion(s), Philosophy of Religion, Religion and Art, Religion and Music, Religion and Literature, Religion and Classics

Types of publications: Essay/Lecture Collections, Reprints, Academic Reference

Ashgate's religious studies program focuses on a broad historical period ranging from late antiquity through the Renaissance. Various books examine a wide variety of historical topics in religion, especially its social impact.

In print: 50 titles.   1997: 15 titles.

ISBN Prefix(es): 0-86078

MS guidelines free upon request & on web site

Preferred form of initial contact: Proposal package containing short query, outline, sample chapters, and recent C.V.

Send submissions to—

John Smedley, Publisher

Limitations/Restrictions: Please, no manuscripts on initial contact.

Complete list of titles available at http://www.ashgate.com.

13   Augsburg Books

Imprint of Augsburg Fortress Publishers

PO Box 1209, Minneapolis, MN 55440

Phone: 612-330-3433

Fax: 612-330-3215

WWW homepage: www.ecla.org/afp/afphome.html

Editorial Director: Dr. Henry F. French

Senior Editor: Ronald Klug

Acquisitions Editor: Robert Klausmeier

Faith/denominational/cultural focus: Interfaith, Ecumenical

Subject areas: Spiritual Life/Personal Religion, Religion and the Family, Religion and Health, Religion in Popular Culture/Media, Religious Education — Elementary

Types of publications: Classroom Instructional Materials, Illustrated Books, Devotional Guides, General Interest Nonfiction — Adult, General Interest Nonfiction — Juvenile, Self-Help, Fiction — Juvenile

Augsburg Books, an imprint of Augsburg Fortress Publishers, the publishing house of the Evangelical Lutheran Church in America, aims to publish for general readers, both Christians and others, whose spiritual questions lead to reflection on Christian tradition or meaning, wholeness, and community. Though topics range broadly, Augsburg Books publishes in some specific categories: spirituality, interactive family books, grief, healing and wholeness, and picture or reference/resource books for children.

In print: 300 titles.   1997: 24 titles.

ISBN Prefix(es): 0-8066

Recent/Forthcoming Titles: Alan Loy McGuinness, *The Balanced Life*; Walter Wangerin, *Probity Jones*; Scott Walker, *Glimpses of God*

Manuscript guidelines free upon request

Preferred form of initial contact: Short written query.

14   Ave Maria Press, Inc

PO Box 428, Notre Dame, IN 46556-0428

Phone: 219-287-2831

Fax: 219-239-2904

Editorial Director: Robert Hamma

Marketing Director: Patrick McGeary

Faith/denominational/cultural focus: Roman Catholic

Subject areas: Liturgy and Ritual, Prayer & Meditation, Vocational/Pastoral Guidance, Spiritual Life/Personal Religion, Religion and the Family, Religion and Health, Religious Biography, Church Issues/Pastoral Practice, Religious Education — Elementary, Religious Education — Secondary

Types of publications: Classroom Instructional Materials, Audio-Visual, Electronic Publications (CD-ROM), General Interest Nonfiction — Adult

Ave Maria Press, Inc., is a Catholic publishing company serving the spiritual and formative needs of Christian individuals, families, the church, and its ministers, and all others seeking spiritual nourishment throughout the world. Our program, which publishes about 35 books and audio programs a year, focuses on such areas as prayer and spirituality, catechesis, parish resources, and pastoral care.

1997: 35 titles.

Recent/Forthcoming Titles: Henri J. M. Nouwen, *Can You Drink the Cup?*; Thomas Merton, *Springs of Contemplation*; Joyce Rupp, *The Cup of Our Life*

Manuscript guidelines free upon request with SASE

Preferred form of initial contact: Proposal package containing SASE, outline, and 2 sample chapters.

15   Baker Academic
Subsidiary/division of Baker Book House Co
PO Box 6287, Grand Rapids, MI 49516-6287
Shipping: 6030 Fulton Road, Ada, MI 49301
Phone: 616-676-9185, 616-676-2315 (editorial)
Fax: 616-676-9573
WWW homepage: www.bakerbooks.com
President: Dwight Baker
Director of Publications: Allan Fisher
Director of Acad. Marketing: Jim Kinney
Faith/denominational/cultural focus: Evangelical Protestant
Subject areas: Prayer & Meditation, Vocational/Pastoral Guidance, Preaching & Homiletics, Missions, Spiritual Life/Personal Religion, Religion and the Family, Ethics, Systematic Theology, Pastoral Theology, Biblical Theology and Biblical Studies, Religion and Literature, Religion and Gender Studies, Psychology of Religion, Religion and Archaeology, Biblical Literature — Commentary & Hermeneutics
Types of publications: Classroom Instructional Materials, Electronic Publications (CD-ROM), Scholarly Monographs, General Reference, Language Reference, Academic Reference
Baker Academic provides resources for students, scholars, and libraries affiliated with religious higher education. Our titles reflect the company's evangelical heritage and express the diversity of that movement. Baker Academic offers textbooks, reference works, and monographs reflecting the highest quality in scholarship, presentation, and production.
Acquisitions focus for 1998-9: Primary textbooks, scholarly monographs and reference works.
In print: 750 titles.   1997: 35 titles.
ISBN Prefix(es): 0-8010
Recent/Forthcoming Titles: Walter Elwell & Robert Yarbrough, *Encountering the New Testament: A Historical and Theological Survey*; Mark Noll, *Turning Points: Decisive Moments in the History of Christianity*; Takamitsu Muraoka, *Hebrew-Aramaic Index to the Septuagint*
MS guidelines free upon request & from web site.
Preferred form of initial contact: Proposal package containing SASE, outline, introduction & 2-3 sample chapters, résumé, and answers to questions in manuscript guidelines.

Send submissions to:
  Biblical studies, theology, reference, textbooks, and monographs: Jim
    Weaver, Editorial Director/Baker Academic
  Religious Education: Bob Hosack, Editor
Limitations/Restrictions: No phone calls please. Queries via e-mail are
    accepted, but not formal proposals.

16   Baker Books Division

Subsidiary/division of Baker Book House Co
PO Box 6287, Grand Rapids, MI 49516-6287
Phone: 616-676-9185
Fax: 616-676-9573
WWW homepage: www.bakerbooks.com
President: Dwight Baker
Dir. of Publications: Allan Fisher
Marketing Director: Joe Tremblay
Publicity Director: Twila Bennett
Sales Manager: Kin Millen
Faith/denominational/cultural focus: Evangelical Protestant
Subject areas: Vocational/Pastoral Guidance, Preaching & Homiletics,
    Spiritual Life/Personal Religion, Religion and the Family, Religion
    and Health, Religious Biography, Religion in Popular
    Culture/Media, Religion and Law, Religion and Public Policy
Types of publications: Books-on-Tape, Reprints, Devotional Guides,
    Fiction — Adult, Self-Help, Fiction — Juvenile
Baker Books appropriate the teachings of God's Word, the Bible, to
    enable individuals and families to develop a vibrant and discerning
    commitment to their Lord, each other, their churches, and their
    community, nation, and world. Books are also published for pastoral
    staff, lay church leaders, and para-church workers to equip them for
    Christ-honoring ministry in a changing world.
1997: 85 titles.
ISBN Prefix(es): 0-8010
Recent/Forthcoming Titles: R. C. Sproul, *Grace Unknown*; John &
    Sylvia Ronsvalle, *Beyond the Stained Glass Windows*; Augusta
    Trobaugh, *Praise Jerusalem!*
MS guidelines free upon request and from web site.

Preferred form of initial contact: Proposal package containing SASE, outline, 2-3 sample chapters, résumé, and answers to questions in MS guidelines.

Send submissions to—

Nonfiction: Robert Hosack, Editor

Fiction: Jane Schrier, Asst. Editor

Professional books: Paul Engle, Editor

Limitations/Restrictions: No e-mail submissions or phone queries accepted.

Do no send the entire manuscript unless specifically requested.

17   Bantam Doubleday Dell

Subsidiary/division of Doubleday

1540 Broadway, New York, NY 10036

Phone: 212-354-6500

Fax: 212-302-7985, 212-782-8911 (Religion Department)

WWW homepage: www.bdd.com

Subject areas: Liturgy and Ritual, Prayer & Meditation, Vocational/Pastoral Guidance, Spiritual Life/Personal Religion, Religion and the Family, Religion and Health, Religious Biography, Religious Thought/Theology, Religious Studies, Religion in Popular Culture/Media, Sacred Literature (including the *New Jerusalem Bible*)

Types of publications: Essay/Lecture Collections, Reprints, Devotional Guides, General Interest Nonfiction — Adult, Translations, Self-Help, Scholarly Monographs, General Reference, Academic Reference

Doubleday's religious titles include classics of religious thought from authors such as Pope John Paul II, Henri Nouwen, and Desmond Tutu; a strong list of religious biography; guides to faith and practice; and the Anchor Bible series of scriptural commentaries. At the heart of our program is the Image Books list (edited by Trace Murphy) featuring the finest in religious paperback publishing, from a new translation of Julian of Norwich's *Revelation of Love* to Thomas Bokenkotter's new *Concise History of the Catholic Church*. During the past year we have increased the strength and diversity of our list by publishing a range of titles specifically for Christian evangelical readers. Our paperback list will further expand in June 1998 with the relaunching of the Galilee imprint. In addition, the next year will see further expansions to the Anchor Bible series and

the first volumes of the new Doubleday Bible Commentaries, a
popular series written by distinguished Bible experts from all areas
In print: 250 titles.   1997: 30 titles.
ISBN Prefix(es): 0-385
Recent/Forthcoming Titles: Heather Whitestone, *Listening with My
    Heart*; Luis Palau, *God is Relevant*; Linda Grenz, *Doubleday Pocket
    Bible Guide*
No manuscript guidelines available
Preferred form of initial contact: Proposal package containing short
    written query & SASE (agented submissions receive preference).
Send submissions to—
    Biblical/general religious titles: Mark Fretz, Senior Editor
    Buddhism, Catholic & Christian titles: Trace Murphy, Editor
    General religious : Eric Major, VP & Director of Religious Publishing

18   Baylor University Press
PO Box 97363, Baylor University, Waco, TX 76798
Phone: 254-755-3217, 254-755-3164 (editorial), 254-755-2161 (orders)
Fax: 254-755-3440, 254-755-2165 (orders)
E-mail: David_Holcomb@baylor.edu
WWW homepage: www.baylor.edu
Academic Publishing Coordinator: Janet Burton
Subject areas: Ethics, Systematic Theology, Theological Education
    (methodology), Faith and Learning, History of Religion(s),
    Philosophy of Religion, Religion and Art, Religion and Music,
    Religion and Gender Studies, Religion and Political Science, Religion
    and Law, Religion and Public Policy, Religious Education — Public
    Policy/Legal Issues
Types of publications: Scholarly Monographs
Baylor University Press publishes contemporary and historical works in
    religious studies, including theology, history of religion, ethics, and
    church-state studies.
Acquisitions focus for 1998-9: Issues in faith and learning, religious
    history, and church-state relations.
In print: 7 titles. 1997: 1 title.
MS guidelines individually discussed
Preferred form of initial contact: Proposal package containing outline
    and 1-3 sample chapters.
Send submissions to—
    J. David Holcomb, Acquisitions Editor

19   Beacon Press

25 Beacon St, Boston, MA 02108-2892
Phone: 617-742-2110
Fax: 617-723-3097
WWW homepage: www.beacon.org/Beacon
Director: Helene Atwan
Faith/denominational/cultural focus: Unitarian Universalist (but also all Christianity, Judaism, Buddhism, feminist spirituality & Africa-derived religions)
Subject areas: Prayer & Meditation, Spiritual Life/Personal Religion, Religion and the Family, Ethics, Pluralistic/Ecumenical Theology, Comparative Religions, History of Religion(s), Religion and Cultural/Ethnic Studies, Religion and Gender Studies, Sociology of Religion, Anthropology of Religion, Religion and Economics, Religion and Political Science, Religion in Popular Culture/Media, Religion and Law, Religion and Public Policy
Types of publications: Essay/Lecture Collections, General Interest Nonfiction — Adult, Scholarly Monographs
Beacon's religion program focuses on progressive works of scholarship that are accessible to the general reader. Our areas of interest include feminist, Goddess, and pagan spirituality, as well as Catholicism, Protestantism, Judaism, and Buddhism; gay and lesbian spirituality, Native American, African-American, and African diasporic religions; comparative religion and Unitarian Universalist perspectives. Our books seek to illuminate knowledge of America's religious past and present; promote the quest for justice, equality, and a sustainable way of life; and deepen the individual's search for faith, truth, and meaning.
Acquisitions focus for 1998-9: In addition to the areas above, Beacon seeks to expand publication of works in Latino/a theology, Asian-American religion, Islam (especially women, Africans, and African-Americans in Islam), and African-American theology.
In print: 78 titles.   1997: 7 titles.
ISBN Prefix(es): 0-8070
Recent/Forthcoming Titles: *Dancing After the Whirlwind: Feminist Reflections on Sex, Denial and Spiritual Transformation*; *Sex and the Church: Gender, Homosexuality and the Transformation of Christian Ethics*; *Opening the Lotus: A Woman's Guide to Buddhism*
Manuscript guidelines free upon request

Preferred form of initial contact: Query letter or proposal package containing SASE, outline and (if included) no more than 1 or 2 sample chapters
Send submissions to—
Susan G. Worst, Editor

20   Bear & Company Publishing
Subsidiary/division of Bear & Co
PO Box 2860, Santa Fe, NM 87504-2860
Phone: 505-983-5968
Fax: 505-989-8386
E-mail: bearco@bearco.com
President: Gerry Clow
Exec. Vice President: Barbara Hand Clow
Treasurer: Diane Winters
VP, Marketing: Jody Winters
Sales Manager: Rob Meadows
Faith/denominational/cultural focus: Creation Spirituality, Native American Spirituality
Subject areas: Spiritual Life/Personal Religion, Religion and Cultural/Ethnic Studies Indigenous Studies, Religion and Gender Studies, Sociology of Religion, Religion and Metaphysics
Types of publications: General Interest Nonfiction — Adult, Self-Help
We publish the works of saints and mystics who took a life-positive view of Creation, particularly Hildegard von Bingen, but also Meister Eckhart, Teilhard de Chardin and the contemporary Matthew Fox. We have a "Meditations with . . ." series which covers Christian mystics and Native American spirituality.
Acquisitions focus for 1998-9: Emphasis on indigenous spirituality more than Christianity.
In print: 15 titles.   1997: 1 title.
ISBN Prefix(es): 0-939680, 1-879181
Recent/Forthcoming Titles: *Medicine Cards Just for Today*
Manuscript guidelines free upon request
Preferred form of initial contact: Proposal package containing query letter, manuscript and SASE.
Send submissions to—
John Nelson, Acquisitions Editor
Limitations/Restrictions: Submissions must contain SASE to be returned.

21 Behrman House
235 Watchung Ave, West Orange, NJ 07052
Phone: 201-669-0447
Fax: 201-669-9769
President: David Behrman
Vice President: Ruby Strauss
Faith/denominational/cultural focus: Judaism
Subject areas: Liturgy and Ritual, Spiritual Life/Personal Religion, Ethics, Religious Education — Elementary, Religious Education — Secondary, Religious Education — Adult
Types of publications: Classroom Instructional Materials, General Reference
Acquisitions focus for 1998-9: Textbooks and trade Judaica
In print: 250 titles.   1997: 10 titles.
ISBN Prefix(es): 0-87441
Recent/Forthcoming Titles: Bradley Artson, *It's a Mitzvah*; Gila Gevirtz, *Partners with God*
No manuscript guidelines available
Preferred form of initial contact: Proposal package containing SASE, outline, 2-3 sample chapters.
Send submissions to—
Adam Siegel, Editor
Limitations/Restrictions: Make sure submission has Jewish content.

22 Bhaktivedanta Book Trust
9710 Venice Blvd #3, Los Angeles, CA 90034
Phone: 800-927-4152
Fax: 310-837-1056
WWW homepage: www.harekrishna.com/ara/
President: Emil Beca
Vice President: John Gunn
Vice President: Stuart Kadetz
Secretary: Gilbert Sanchez
Faith/denominational/cultural focus: Vedic literatures
Subject areas: Prayer & Meditation, Missions, Religious Biography, Comparative Religions, History of Religion(s), Philosophy of Religion, Religion in Popular Culture/Media, Tantric/Vedic Lit. — Translations
Types of publications: Translations

We carry the ancient literatures of Gaudiya Vaisnava Hinduism, as translated by His Divine Grace A. C. Bhaktivedanta Swami Prabhupada.
In print: 30 titles.
ISBN Prefix(es): 89213
Recent/Forthcoming Titles: *Mahabharat Quest for Enlightenment*; *Dharma*; *Vision for the New Millenium*
No manuscript guidelines available
No unsolicited submissions accepted

23   Blackwell Publishers Ltd
108 Cowley Road, Oxford OX4 IJF United Kingdom
Orders (UK): Marston Book Services, PO Box 269, Abingdon, Oxon OX14 4YN; Orders (US):, AIDC, PO Box 20, Williston, VT 05495-0020
Phone: +44-1865-791100
Fax: +44-1865-791347
WWW homepage: blackwellpublishers.co.uk
Subject areas: Liturgy and Ritual, Religious Thought/Theology, Religious Studies, Religion and Society, Religious Education
Types of publications: Classroom Instructional Materials, Electronic Publications (CD-ROM and disk-based products), Academic Reference
Blackwell Publishers publish books for students, both undergraduate and postgraduate. We pride ourselves on our thorough theology and religious studies publishing program; our authors include Alister McGrath and John Milbank. Our publishing focus includes publishing texts, anthologies, and reference works which will be used in teaching throughout the world.
Acquisitions focus for 1998-9: Theology, Biblical and religious studies.
In print: 100+ titles.   1997: 15 titles.
ISBN Prefix(es): 0-631; 1-55786
Recent/Forthcoming Titles: McGrath, *Christian Theology: An Introduction (2nd ed.)*; Don Cupitt, *Mysticism After Modernity*; Graham Ward, *The Postmodern God: A Theological Reader*
Manuscript guidelines free upon request
Preferred form of initial contact: Short written query
Send submissions to—
    Martin Davies, Editor
    Stephan Chambers, Editorial Director

24   Bluestar Communications
44 Bear Glenn, Woodside, CA 94062
Phone: 415-851-5880
Fax: 415-851-2333
E-mail: orders@bluestar.com
WWW homepage: www.bluestar.com
CEO: Petra Michel
CFO: A. Richard Newton
Sales & Warehouse: Christopher Smith
Faith/denominational/cultural focus: New Age
Subject areas: Religious Biography, Doctrinal Theology & Dogma, Comparative Religions, Mythology, Buddhist Literature — Commentary & Hermeneutics
Types of publications: Music, Illustrated Books, General Interest Nonfiction — Adult, Fiction — Adult, Self-Help
In print: 10 titles.   1997: 3 titles.
ISBN Prefix(es): 1-885394
Recent/Forthcoming Titles: Ute York, *Living by the Moon*; Dalai Lama, *Buddha Nature*; Peter Michel, *Faith & Dogma*
Preferred form of initial contact:

25   Bolchazy-Carducci Publishers, Inc
1000 Brown Street, Unit 101, Wauconda, IL 60084
Phone: 847-526-4344
Fax: 847-526-2867
E-mail: latin@bolchazy.com
WWW homepage: www.bolchazy.com
President: Ladislaus J. Bolchazy, Ph.D.
Vice President: Marie Bolchazy, Ph.D.
Faith/denominational/cultural focus: Ancient Religions
Subject areas: Comparative Religions, History of Religion(s), Mythology, Religion and Classics, Anthropology of Religion
Types of publications: Music, Translations, Language Reference, Academic Reference, Concordances
Our titles in this category include ancient classics, Greek & Latin texts, and books on the history of ethical and theological concepts, comparative religions, and mythologies of the Western world, as well as music.
In print: 10 titles.   1997: 2 titles.

ISBN Prefix(es): 0-86516
Send $1.01 in postage on 9x12 envelope for MS guidelines
Preferred form of initial contact: Proposal package containing SASE,
   outline, at least 3 sample chapters, and author C.V.
Send submissions to—
   Ladislaus J. Bolchazy, Ph.D., President
Limitations/Restrictions: Proposal should include analysis of and
   comparison with existing titles and list of features: bibliography,
   glossary, illustrations, etc.
We will request full manuscripts after review of proposal and sample,
   when appropriate.

26   Brill Academic Publishers
Plantijnstraat 2, 2321 JC, PO Box 9000, 23200 PA, Leiden, The
   Netherlands
US Headquarters: 24 Hudson St, PO Box 467, Kinderhook, NY 12106
Phone: 3171-5353500, 518-758-1411 (US Headquarters)
Fax: 3171-537532, 518-758-1959 (US Headquarters (fax))
E-mail: cs@brill.nl
Account Manager (U.S.): Ellen Endres
Sales Manager (NL): Pieter Gispen
Subject areas: Missions, Ethics, Pluralistic/Ecumenical Theology,
   Comparative Religions, History of Religion(s), Interdisciplinary
   Studies, Philosophy of Religion, Religion and Art, Religion and
   Music, Religion and Literature, Religion and Classics, Religion and
   Cultural/Ethnic Studies, Religion and Gender Studies, Sociology of
   Religion, Anthropology of Religion, Religion and Archaeology,
   Religion in Popular Culture/Media, Biblical Literature —
   Commentary & Hermeneutics, Biblical Literature — Philology &
   Linguistics, Biblical Literature — Cultural & Historical Contexts,
   Biblical Literature — Translations, Talmudic Literature —
   Commentary & Hermeneutics, Talmudic Literature — Philology &
   Linguistics, Talmudic Literature — Cultural & Historical Contexts,
   Talmudic Literature — Translations, Koranic Literature —
   Commentary & Hermeneutics, Koranic Literature — Philology &
   Linguistics, Koranic Literature — Cultural & Historical Contexts,
   Koranic Literature — Translations, Tantric/Vedic Literature —
   Translations, Buddhist Literature — Translations

Types of publications: Electronic Publications (CD-ROM; microfiche), Essay/Lecture Collections, Scholarly Monographs, Dissertations, Academic Reference

Journals and monograph series in Biblical studies, religion in antiquity, Judaism, early Christianity, Gnosticism, Islam, Oriental religions, Graeco-Roman religions, religion in Africa, Dead Sea Scrolls, religion and the arts, missiology, ecumenical studies, apocrypha and pseudipigrapha, ancient Near Eastern studies, history of religions, Manichaeism, hermeneutics, Semitic philology, and the history of Christian thought.

Acquisitions focus for 1998-9: Journals and reference works in Biblical studies; religion and the arts; theology.

In print: 860 titles.   1997: 75 titles.

5% of titles author-subsidized

ISBN Prefix(es): 9-004

Recent/Forthcoming Titles: W. W. Halo (ed.), *The Context of Scripture*; S. E. Porter (ed.), *Handbook of New Testament Exegesis*; T. H. Lim, *The Dead Sea Scrolls Electronic Reference Library (CD-ROM)*

Manuscript guidelines free upon request

Preferred form of initial contact: Proposal package containing outline and 2 sample chapters.

Send submissions to—

Biblical studies (NT), missiology, religions in Africa, Gnosticism: D. E. Orton

Biblical studies (OT), Dead Sea Scrolls, history of religions: J. M. Van Der Meij

Islam: P. Bearman

Ancient Near East/Orient: A. Hoffstaedt

27   Buddhist Books International

Subsidiary/division of Buddhist Books International of Japan

Eikyoji Shigai 56 Tadoshi, Fukagawa, Hokkaido 071 Japan

U.S. Mailing and Orders: Buddhist Books International, c/o Reno Buddhist Church, 820 Plumas St, Reno, NV 89509

Phone: +81-1642-7-2403, 702-348-6603 (U.S. office)

Fax: +81-1642-2511

President: Bhadra Holm

Director: Daigan Matsunaga

Director: Alicia Matsunaga

Exec. Secretary: Ruth Delegado
Shipping Manager: Harutoshi Imai
Faith/denominational/cultural focus: Buddhism
Subject areas: Spiritual Life/Personal Religion, Systematic Theology,
    Pluralistic/Ecumenical Theology, Religion in Popular Culture &
    Media, Buddhist Literature — Translations
Types of publications: Essay/Lecture Collections, Translations, Poetry,
    Scholarly Monographs, Academic Reference
The aims of our press are to promote the study and understandings of
    Buddhism in a philosophical and historical context, as well as to
    foster the relationship between Buddhism and other religions.
Acquisitions focus for 1998-9: Poetry, sermons, systematic theology.
In print: 2 titles. 1997: 1 title.
Recent/Forthcoming Titles: *Broken Light* (ecumenical poetry);
    Collection of Buddhist Sermons; The Theology of Assimilation
Manuscript guidelines free upon request
Preferred form of initial contact: Proposal package containing outline.
    No unsolicited submissions.
Send submissions to—
    Ruth Delegado, Executive Secretary
Acquisitions address: 820 Plumas St, Reno, NV 89509

28   The American Institute for Patristic & Byzantine Studies
12 Minuet Lane, Kingston, NY 12401
The Patristic & Byzantine Rev.: RR 1 Box 353-A, Kingston, NY 12401
Phone: 914-336-8797
Faith/denominational/cultural focus: Eastern Orthodox
Subject areas: Pluralistic/Ecumenical Theology, Philosophy of Religion,
    Biblical Literature — Philology & Linguistics, Biblical Literature —
    Cultural & Historical Contexts, Biblical Literature — Translations,
    Religious Education — Seminary
Types of publications: Essay/Lecture Collections, Scholarly
    Monographs, Dissertations
The American Institute for Patristic & Byzantine Studies publishes
    works of theology, philosophy, sociology, and psychotherapy in
    Eastern Church Fathers. Anthropology and political theology in
    Byzantine civilization. Human rights and socio-political values in
    Greek Christianity and philosophy.
In print: 22 titles.   1997: 3 titles.

Recent/Forthcoming Titles: *Byzantine Humanist Scholarship; Byzantine Forerunners of the Italian Renaissance; Byzantine Humanism and HESYCHASM*
Preferred form of initial contact: Short written query with outline.

29   Cambridge University Press

Cambridge University Press, Publishing Division, Shaftesbury Road, Cambridge, CB2 2RU United Kingdom
North American Branch: 40 West 20th St, New York, NY 10011-4211
Phone: +44-1223-312393, 212-924-3900 (U.S. office)
Fax: +44-1223-315052, 212-691-3239 (U.S. office)
E-mail: information@cup.cam.ac.uk (UK) / @cup.org (USA)
WWW homepage: www.cup.cam.ac.uk
Subject areas: Ethics, Doctrinal Theology & Dogma, Process Theology, Systematic Theology, Pastoral Theology, Theological Education (methodology), Pluralistic/Ecumenical Theology, Comparative Religions, History of Religion(s), Sacred Languages, Philosophy of Religion, Religion and Literature, Religion and Classics, Religion and Cultural/Ethnic Studies, Religion and Gender Studies, Psychology of Religion, Sociology of Religion, Anthropology of Religion, Religion and Archaeology, Religion and Economics, Religion in Popular Culture/Media, Religion and Law, Religion and Public Policy, Sacred Literature — Commentary & Hermeneutics, Sacred Literature — Philology & Linguistics, Sacred Literature — Cultural & Historical Contexts, Religious Education — Theory and Methodology, Religious Education — Seminary, Religious Education — Adult
Types of publications: Classroom Instructional Materials, Essay/Lecture Collections, Scholarly Monographs, Language Reference, Academic Reference
Cambridge University Press serves the research and teaching activities of the academic world through the publication of books and journals in the English language. Our books in religion cover every aspect of the subject: Biblical studies, theology, philosophy of religion, Jewish studies, religious studies, etc. We publish at a variety of levels, from introductory textbooks for students to scholarly research monographs (most of which are published in series) and academic reference volumes. Publishing between 25 and 35 titles each year, we are committed to keeping our books in print for as long as possible,

and to distributing them internationally through our offices and agents worldwide.

Acquisitions focus for 1998-9: Although we remain committed to our academic monograph publications, in 1998 and 1999 we will be concentrating on expanding our list of books for students, and on adding to our academic reference titles. Current plans include further "Introductions to religions," *Cambridge Companions* to Religion (edited collections of commissioned essays), textbooks in Biblical studies, and the *Cambridge Histories* of Christianity and Judaism.

In print: 454 titles.   1997: 27 titles.

ISBN Prefix(es): 0-521

Recent/Forthcoming Titles: Colin Gunton, ed., *Cambridge Companion to Christian Doctrine* (0-521-47695x); Gavin Flood, *Introduction to Hinduism* (0-521-438780); David Parker, *The Living Text of the Gospels* (0-521-599512)

See WWW page for manuscript guidelines.

Preferred form of initial contact: Proposal package containing outline and short C.V.

Send submissions to—
    Ruth Paar

Cambridge Univ. Press publishes worldwide (i.e. we do not do co-publications w/U.S. publishers). We have offices and agents in Europe, N. & S. America, Australia, S. & E. Asia, and Africa.

30   Canon Law Society of America

Canon Law Society of America, Catholic University, 431 Caldwell, Washington, DC 20064

Phone: 202-269-3491

Fax: 202-319-5719

E-mail: clsa@tidalwave.net

WWW homepage: www.clsa.org

Exec. Coordinator: Patrick Cogan

Faith/denominational/cultural focus: Roman Catholic

Subject areas: Canon Law

Types of publications: Proceedings, Marriage Tribunal Studies

CLSA publishes studies in canon law, the discipline of the Roman Catholic Church. Studies for publications are produced via commissioned works or committee activity.

In print: 49 titles.   1997: 4 titles.

ISBN Prefix(es): 0-943616

Recent/Forthcoming Titles: *Roman Replies and CLSA Advisory Opinions 1997; Proceedings 1996; Marriage Jurisprudence*

No manuscript guidelines available

No unsolicited submissions accepted

31   William Carey Library

1705 North Sierra Bonita Ave, Pasadena, CA 91104

Mailing: PO Box 40129, Pasadena, CA 91114

Phone: 626-798-0819, 800-777-6371 (toll free), 800-647-7466 (toll free)

Fax: 626-798-0819

General Partner: Ralph D. Winter

General Manager: Ernest von Seggern

Faith/denominational/cultural focus: Evangelical Christian

Subject areas: Missions, Religious Biography, Theological Education (Methodology), Comparative Religions, Religion and Cultural/Ethnic Studies, Anthropology of Religion, Religion in Popular Culture/Media, Biblical Literature — Commentary & Hermeneutics, Sacred Literature — Philology & Linguistics, Religious Education — Seminary, Missionary Training

Types of publications: Classroom Instructional Materials, Essay/Lecture Collections, Reprints, Scholarly Monographs, Dissertations

Founded for the exclusive purpose of publishing at reasonable cost the best in current thinking on missions of all denominations, cultures, and nations. It is our aim to aid the work of the mission executive, the missionary in the field and his home church, and the student of mission.

In print: 104 titles.   1997: 11 title.

ISBN Prefix(es): 0-87808

Recent/Forthcoming Titles: *Research in Church and Mission; Communicating Christ in an Animistic Context; Then the End Will Come*

Manuscript guidelines free upon request

Preferred form of initial contact: Proposal package containing short query, SASE, outline, and author profile.

Send submissions to—

Jone Bosch, Review Editor

32   Catholic Health Association of the United States
4455 Woodson Rd, St. Louis, MO 63134-3797
Phone: 314-253-3445
Fax: 314-253-3540
WWW homepage: www.chausa.org
Senior Associate: Robert J. Stephens
Faith/denominational/cultural focus: Roman Catholic
Subject areas: Liturgy and Ritual, Religion and Health, Religious
    Biography, Ethics, Pastoral Theology, Religion in Popular
    Culture/Media, Religion and Law, Religion and Public Policy,
    Religious Education — Public policy/Legal Issues
Types of publications: Audio-Visual, Electronic Publications (World
    Wide Web), Scholarly Monographs
The Catholic Health Association publishes works on health care ethics;
    ministry and health care; mission and health care; public policy,
    religion, ethics and health care; health care advocacy.
In print: 30+ titles.   1997: 10 titles.
ISBN Prefix(es): 0-87125
No manuscript guidelines available
Preferred form of initial contact: Short written query
Send submissions to—
    Robert J. Stephen, Senior Associate

33   The Catholic News Publishing Company
210 North Avenue, New Rochelle, NY 10801
Phone: 914-632-1220
Fax: 914-632-3412
Sales Manager: Thomas White
Editor: Mari Castrovilla
Editor: Annette Miserendino
Faith/denominational/cultural focus: Roman Catholic
We publish two resources for Roman Catholics: *A Guide to Religious
    Ministries* and *The Catholic Telephone Guide.*
No manuscript guidelines available
No unsolicited submissions accepted

34   Chosen Books
Subsidiary/division of Baker Book House
PO Box 6287, Grand Rapids, MI 49516-6287
Phone: 616-676-9185
Fax: 616-676-9573
WWW homepage: www.bakerbooks.com
Faith/denominational/cultural focus: Evangelical Protestant
Subject areas: Prayer & Meditation, Spiritual Life/Personal Religion
Types of publications: Devotional Guides
Chosen Books publishes about ten books per year. Our goal is to publish well-crafted books that recognize the gifts and ministry of the Holy Spirit and help the reader live a more empowered and effective life for Jesus Christ.
In print: 100 titles.   1997: 10 titles.
ISBN Prefix(es): 0-80079
Recent/Forthcoming Titles: Charles Kraft, *I Give You Authority*; Bob Beckett, *Commitment to Conquer*; Signa Bodishbaugh, *The Journey to Wholeness in Christ*
Manuscript guidelines free upon request (and from web site)
Preferred form of initial contact: Short written query
Send submissions to—
    Jane Campbell, Editor

35   Christian Publications Inc
3825 Hartzdale Drive, Camp Hill, PA 17011
Phone: 717-761-7044, 800-233-4443 (orders)
Fax: 717-761-7273
WWW homepage: cpi-horizon.com
Publisher: K. Neil Foster
VP Marketing/Sales: William R. Goetz
Controller: Rick Evans
Editorial Director: George McPeek
Faith/denominational/cultural focus: Evangelical Christian (The Christian & Missionary Alliance)
Subject areas: Prayer & Meditation, Preaching & Homiletics, Missions, Spiritual Life/Personal Religion, Religion and the Family, Religion and Health, Religious Biography, Pastoral Theology, Biblical Literature — Commentary & Hermeneutics

Types of publications: Books-on-Tape, Essay/Lecture Collections, Reprints, Devotional Guides, Fiction — Adult, Fiction — Juvenile

The purpose of Christian Publications is to propagate the Gospel of Jesus Christ, as outlined in The Christian & Missionary Alliance statement of faith, particularly the message of Jesus Christ, Our Savior, Sanctifier, Healer and Coming King, to the Alliance constituency, as well as to the broader evangelical community worldwide, and to unbelievers. This is done by evangelistic, deeper life, and other publishing.

Acquisitions focus for 1998-9: Looking for authors with a flair for contemporary writing styles to communicate the above messages.

In print: 300 titles.   1997: 30 titles.

5% of titles author-subsidized

ISBN Prefix(es): 0-87509, 0-88965 (Horizon imprint)

Recent/Forthcoming Titles: *Out of the Locker Room of the Male Soul*; *Disney and the Bible*; *The Attributes of God*

Manuscript guidelines free upon request

Preferred form of initial contact: Proposal package containing SASE, outline, and sample chapters.

Send submissions to—

George McPeek, Editorial Director

Limitations/Restrictions: No poetry and very limited children's books.

Author's should be prepared to submit final manuscript on computer disk (if accepted).

36   Church and Synagogue Library Association

PO Box 19357, Portland, OR 97280-0357

Phone: 503-244-6919, 800-542-2752

Fax: 503-977-3734

E-mail: csla@worldaccessnet.com

WWW homepage: www.worldaccessnet.com/~csla

Faith/denominational/cultural focus: Interfaith

No manuscript guidelines available

No unsolicited submissions accepted

37   Clarity Press, Inc
3277 Roswell Rd, NE, Suite 469, Atlanta, GA 30305
Phone: 404-231-0649
Fax: 404-231-3899, 306-789-0474
E-mail: clarity@islandnet.com
WWW homepage: www.bookmasters.com/clarity
Editorial Director: Diana G. Collier
Business Manager: Annette Gordon
Subject areas: Liberation Theology, Religion and Economics, Religion and Political Science, Religion and Social Concerns, Religion and Public Policy, Religion and Human Rights
Types of publications: General Interest Nonfiction — Adult (trade paperback)
Clarity Press is a nonsectarian publisher of quality titles on human rights issues. Manuscripts addressing contemporary social issues within the context of religious beliefs are acceptable; the primary emphasis should be to shed new light on the social (human rights) issue itself through a scholarly, well-documented presentation. The MS may indicate a religion's tenets as exemplary in the promotion of human justice, or it may critique the socio-political effects of a religion as practiced. Overall, the title must seek to further peaceful, just, and equitable socio-economical and political relations between individuals, groups, and nations. We are not interested in strictly theological/philosophical works interpreting specific or general principles of a religion.
In print: 2 titles. 1997: 1 title.
ISBN Prefix(es): 0-932863
Recent/Forthcoming Titles: Thomas L. Are, *Israeli Peace/Palestinian Justice: Liberation Theology and the Peace Process*; Binka LeBreton, *A Land to Die For*
Preferred form of initial contact: Proposal package containing outline, synopsis, table of contents, author's biography, and endorsements.
Limitations/Restrictions: Do not include SASE in proposals; we will respond only if interested.

29

38   College Press Publishing Co

Box 1132, Joplin, MO 64802
Street Address: 223 W 3rd, Joplin, MO 64801
Phone: 800-289-3300
Fax: 417-623-8250
E-mail: collegepress@collegepress.com
WWW homepage: www.collegepress.com
President: Chris DeWelt
Business Manager: Gregg Murdock
Director of Marketing: Steve Cable
Managing Editor: John Hunter
Production Manager: Steve Jennings
Faith/denominational/cultural focus: Christian, Churches of Christ
Subject areas: Prayer & Meditation, Vocational/Pastoral Guidance,
   Preaching & Homiletics, Missions, Ethics, Doctrinal Theology &
   Dogma, Comparative Religions, Philosophy of Religion, Sociology
   of Religion, Religion and the Natural Sciences, Methodologies of
   Study and Teaching, Religion in Popular Culture/Media, Sacred
   Literature — Commentary & Hermeneutics, Religious Education —
   Methodology, Religious Education — Elementary, Religious
   Education — Secondary, Religious Education — Post-Secondary,
   Religious Education — Seminary, Religious Education — Adult
Types of publications: Classroom Instructional Materials,
   Essay/Lecture Collections, Reprints, Devotional Guides, General
   Interest Nonfiction — Adult, Self-Help, Academic Reference
Acquisitions focus for 1998-9: Bible studies that support the motto:
   "Every Christian a Bible student"; conservative works with an
   Arminian perspective and an amillennial eschatology. Exegetical
   studies of Bible texts must reflect serious and defensible positions.
In print: 200 titles.   1997: 24 titles.
.5% of titles author-subsidized
ISBN Prefix(es): 0-89900
Recent/Forthcoming Titles: *Coming Together in Christ*; *Christians on
   the Oregon Trail*; *See the Gods Fall*
Send #10 SASE for manuscript guidelines
Preferred form of initial contact: Short written query
Send submissions to—
   John Hunter, Managing Editor

39   Columbia University Press
562 W 113, New York, NY 10025
Phone: 212-666-1000
Fax: 212-316-3100
WWW homepage: www.columbia.edu/CU/CUP
Director: William Strachan
Subject areas: Religion and Literature, Religion and Cultural/Ethnic
    Studies, Religion and Gender Studies, Religion and Political Science
Types of publications: Electronic Publications (CD-ROM), Scholarly
    Monographs, Academic Reference
Columbia University Press' religion-related list includes scholarly books
    in religion and history, politics, gender, and cultural studies.
In print: 20 titles.   1997: 5 titles.
No manuscript guidelines available
Preferred form of initial contact: Short written query
Send submissions to—
    Literature/literary criticism: Jennifer Creuse, Editor
    Gay & lesbian: Ann Miller, Editor
    History/politics: Kate Wittenberg, Editor

40   Concordia Publishing House
3558 S Jefferson Ave, St. Louis, MO 63118-3968
Phone: 314-268-1000
Fax: 314-268-1329
President & CEO: Rev. Steve Carter
Faith/denominational/cultural focus: Lutheran — Missouri Synod
Subject areas: Preaching, Spiritual Life & Personal Religion, Pastoral
    Theology, Biblical Literature — Commentary & Hermeneutics
Types of publications: Classroom Instructional Materials, Music,
    Illustrated Books, Devotional Guides, Liturgical Materials, General
    Interest Nonfiction — Adult, General Interest Nonfiction —
    Juvenile, Fiction — Juvenile
Most of our publications are contracted by CPH with known authors in
    the Lutheran church. The only area in which we regularly use free-
    lance submissions is children's and family resources and teaching
    resources for Christian classrooms. We publish approximately 80
    titles per year in categories such as picture books, Arch Books, series
    fiction for young readers, devotional products for children and
    adults, practical books for teens and adults, family skills books,

teaching resources, etc. All products for children, adults, and teachers should be Bible-based, Christ-centered, and discuss real-life application of biblical truths. We currently do not publish teen or adult fiction, personal experience, or biography.

Acquisitions focus for 1998-9: We are especially in need of proposals for practical family books, children's activity books, and teaching resources for use in the Christian early childhood or elementary classroom (for publication in 1999-2000).

In print: 539 titles.   1997: 82 titles.

Recent/Forthcoming Titles: *Prime Time Preaching; To the Ends of the Earth; The Pilgrim Path (church drama)*

Send #10 SASE for manuscript guidelines

Preferred form of initial contact: Proposal package containing short query, SASE, outline, and 1-2 sample chapters. No phone queries.

Send submissions to—

Children & family resources: Ruth Geisler, Creative Director

Pastoral theology and practice: Rev. John Nunes, Director

Music resources: Rev. David Johnson, Creative Director

Drama resources: Rachel Hoyer, Editor

Devotional resources: Dawn Weinstock, Editor

Limitations/Restrictions: For music submissions (sacred music only) include SASE for MS return (if rejected). No simultaneous submissions.

41   Contemporary Drama Service

Subsidiary/division of Meriwether Publishing Ltd.

885 Elkton Drive, Colorado Springs, CO 80907-3557

Phone: 719-594-4422

Fax: 719-594-9916

Associate Editor: Rhonda Wray

Faith/denominational/cultural focus: Mainline Protestant churches, non-denominational

Subject areas: Religious Education — Elementary, Religious Education — Secondary

Types of publications: Classroom Instructional Materials, Liturgical Materials, Chancel Drama

We are one of the first, if not the first, publishing house to specialize in chancel drama. Our first church plays were published over 30 years ago. We publish easy-to-stage plays for all Christian holidays and for Christian education for teens and adults throughout the church year. We also publish non-fiction books and dramatic fiction works for use in planning youth activities.

Acquisitions focus for 1998-9: We will be looking for children's Easter and Christmas plays. Other acquisition needs are for church dinner plays, Christmas and Easter musicals, and books of Christian education games.

In print: 26 titles.

ISBN Prefix(es): 1-56608

Recent/Forthcoming Titles: *Issac Air Freight — The Works*; *Fool of the Kingdom: How to be an Effective Clown Minister*

Send $1 for MS guidelines and catalog

Preferred form of initial contact: Short written query for book proposals or proposal package containing SASE, outline, and music cassettes (for musical submissions)

Send submissions to—
    Books: Arthur Zapel, Executive Editor
    Plays & children's scripts: Rhonda Wray, Associate Editor

No submissions or replies returned without SASE.

42   The Continuum Publishing Company

370 Lexington Ave, New York, NY 10017
Phone: 212-953-5858
Fax: 212-953-5944
E-mail: contin@tiac.net
WWW homepage: www.continuum-books.com
Chairman: Werner Mark Linz
President: Gene Gollogly
Executive VP: Ulla Schnell
Managing Editor: Evander Lomke
Promotion Director: Martin Rowe
Faith/denominational/cultural focus: Ecumenical
Subject areas: Prayer & Meditation, Vocational/Pastoral Guidance, Spiritual Life/Personal Religion, Ethics, Systematic Theology, Pastoral Theology, Pluralistic/Ecumenical Theology, Comparative Religions, History of Religion(s), Religion and Art, Religion and Gender Studies, Religion and the Physical Sciences, Religion and Public Policy, Biblical Literature — Commentary & Hermeneutics, Biblical Literature — Cultural & Historical Contexts

Types of publications: Illustrated Books, Essay/Lecture Collections, General Interest Nonfiction — Adult, Scholarly Monographs, General Reference, Academic Reference

Continuum publishes for scholarly, professional, educational, and general trade markets in the areas of ethics, ecotheology, feminist theology, Judaism, Christian origins/New Testament, history of Christianity, contemporary Christian thought, Jewish-Christian relations, African-American theology, world religions, as well as popular spirituality.

In print: 150 titles.   1997: 40 titles.

ISBN Prefix(es): 0-8264

Recent/Forthcoming Titles: Bernard McGinn, John Collins & Stephen Stein, eds., *The Encyclopedia of Apocalypticism*; Heinz Schreckenberg, *The Jews in Christian Art: An Illustrated History*; Elizabeth A. Johnson, *Friends of God and Prophets: A Feminist Theological Reading of the Communion of Saints*

No manuscript guidelines available

Preferred form of initial contact: Proposal package containing SASE, outline, 2 sample chapters, and author's résumé.

Send submissions to—
Frank Oveis, Publishing Director
Justus George Lawler, Academic Editor
Address for J. G. Lawler: PO Box 1370, St. Charles, IL 60174

43   Cornell University Press

Subsidiary/division of Cornell University
Sage House, 512 E State St, Ithaca, NY 14850
Phone: 607-277-2338
Fax: 607-277-2374, 607-277-6292 (orders)

Faith/denominational/cultural focus: Religion of medieval/early modern Europe and modern America (culture of); analytic philosophy of religion

Subject areas: Ethics, History of Religion(s), Mythology, Folklore, Philosophy of Religion, Religion and Literature, Religion and Classics, Religion and Cultural/Ethnic Studies, Religion and Gender Studies, Sociology of Religion, Anthropology of Religion, Religion and Archaeology, Religion and Political Science, Religion and Society, Sacred Literature — Cultural & Historical Contexts

Types of publications: Scholarly Monographs

We seek to publish on the cultural history of religion, focusing on medieval and early modern Europe and modern America. In each of these areas, we also seek studies of literature that are richly contextualized. The history and culture of ancient religions (Egypt, Greece, and Rome) is another focus. We seek to expand our lists on religion and politics in modern Europe (east and west) and to maintain our program in philosophical theology.

Acquisitions focus for 1998-9: Medieval studies, Egyptology and classics, religion in modern America, and the world of Eastern Orthodoxy.

In print: 200 titles.   1997: 20 titles.

ISBN Prefix(es): 0-8014

Recent/Forthcoming Titles: J. F. Nagy, *Conversing with Angels and Ancients*; Shafer, *Temples of Ancient Egypt*; Binski, *Medieval Death*

Manuscript guidelines free upon request

Preferred form of initial contact: Proposal package containing outline, 2 chapters, table of contents, and author's current C.V.

Send submissions to—

Medieval & early modern history, philosophical theology, and Russian history: John G. Ackerman, Director

American history and anthropology: Peter Agree, Editor

Classics, Egyptology, medieval literature, Judaica: Bernhard Kendler, Executive Editor

Politics and religion, Middle Eastern and Asian studies: Roger Haydon, Editor

44   Cornerstone Productions Inc

Subsidiary/division of Reggae Legends

Imprint of Ras Cardo Publishings

PO Box 55229, Atlanta, GA 30308-5229

Phone: 404-288-8937

Pres./Founder: Ricardo Scott J.D.

CEO: Giancarlo R. Scott

Faith/denominational/cultural focus: Rastafarian, Spirituality

Subject areas: Liturgy and Ritual, Prayer & Meditation, Missions, Spiritual Life/Personal Religion, Religion and the Family, Religion and Health, Ethics, Comparative Religions, History of Religion(s), Religion and Music, Religion and Cultural/Ethnic Studies, Religion and Gender Studies, Sociology of Religion, Religion and the Natural

Sciences, Religion and Society, Biblical Literature — Cultural & Historical Contexts, Koranic Literature — Cultural & Historical Contexts, Religious Education

Types of publications: Classroom Instructional Materials, Books-on-Tape, Audio-Visual, Electronic Publications (CD-ROM), Music, Illustrated Books, Essay/Lecture Collections, General Interest Nonfiction — Adult, General Interest Nonfiction — Juvenile, Translations, Self-Help, Poetry, Scholarly Monographs, General Reference, Academic Reference

Ricardo Scott, J.D, AKA Ras Cardo—poet, reggae originator, Rastafarian spiritual writer and musician—is the worlds most prolific cultural icon and pre-eminent authority on Jamaican Rastafarian spiritual practices and principles of life and living. As founder and publisher of Cornerstone Productions, he brings the true facts as to how religion divides us, whereas spirituality unites us.

Acquisitions focus for 1998-9: Using the written or spoken word in reggae and reggae Godlike spirituality to heal the nations of the Earth and save God's children.

In print: 7 titles. 1997: 5 titles.

ISBN Prefix(es): 1-883427

Recent Titles: *Techno-Tyrannical Society*; *R.A.S.P.E.C.T.-1(Jah's Signs and Prophecies)*; *Ricardo's Poetical Works*

Preferred form of initial contact: Proposal package containing SASE, outline, and sample chapters

Send submissions to—

Ricardo Scott J. D., President

Limitations/Restrictions: Submissions must focus on solving ills of the human condition (i.e. poverty, neglect, abuse) with the love of God, and must reflect on life, love, and concern for all of God's creation.

45   Crossroad Publishing Company
Subsidiary/division of Herder Publishing
370 Lexington Ave, New York, NY 10017
Phone: 212-532-3650
Fax: 212-532-4922
E-mail: editor@crossroadpublishing.com
President & CEO: Gwendolin Herder
Exec. VP & Publisher: Michael Leach
Exec. VP & Dir. Marketing/Sales: Robert Byrns
Faith/denominational/cultural focus: Interfaith, Ecumenical Christian

Subject areas: Religious Life/Practice, Religious Thought/Theology, Comparative Religions, History of Religion(s), Mythology, Philosophy of Religion, Religion and Classics, Religion and Cultural/Ethnic Studies, Religion and Gender Studies, Psychology of Religion, Sociology of Religion, Anthropology of Religion, Religion in Popular Culture/Media, Religion and Public Policy, Biblical Literature — Commentary & Hermeneutics, Biblical Literature — Cultural & Historical Contexts, Biblical Literature — Translations, Religious Education — Theory and Methodology, Religious Education — Post-Secondary, Religious Education — Seminary, Religious Education — Adult

Types of publications: Classroom Instructional Materials, Books-on-Tape, Illustrated Books, Essay/Lecture Collections, Reprints, Devotional Guides, Liturgical Materials, General Interest Nonfiction — Adult, Translations, Self-Help, Fiction — Juvenile, Scholarly Monographs, General Reference, Academic Reference

The Crossroad Publishing Company has two imprints: Crossroad and Crossroad/Herder. The Crossroad imprint offers books in religion, spirituality, and personal growth that speak to a wide diversity of backgrounds and beliefs. Its goal is to participate in humankind's quest for meaning through books that inform, enlighten, and heal. The Crossroad/Herder imprint offers a twofold program: books for the academic study of religion and theology, and books for the formation and enrichment of active members of parishes and religious communities in Catholic and mainline Protestant churches. Its goal is to promote the church's ministry by providing books that enhance learning, foster faith, and help build the communities of tomorrow.

In print: 500 titles.   1997: 75 titles.

5% of titles author-subsidized

ISBN Prefix(es): 0-8245

Recent/Forthcoming Titles: Phyllis Tickle, *God Talk in America* (Crossroad Imprint); *The Girard Reader*; *The Catholic Common Ground Initiaive: Foundational Documents* (Crossroad/Herder)

No manuscript guidelines available

Preferred form of initial contact: Proposal package containing SASE, outline, at least 2 sample chapters & author biography. or C.V. Complete MS with proposal and biography, preferred.

Send submissions to—
    Crossroad Imprint: Michael Leach, Publisher
    Crossroad/Herder Imprint: James Le Grys, Academic Editor

46   The Dordt College Press
Subsidiary/division of Dordt College
498 4th Ave NE, Sioux Center, IA 51250
Phone: 712-722-6002, 712-722-6421 (orders)
Fax: 712-722-1185, 712-722-6416 (orders)
E-mail: dordtpress@dordt.edu
WWW homepage: www.dordt.edu/pubs/dordtpress
Faith/denominational/cultural focus: Reformed, Evangelical
Subject areas: Doctrinal Theology & Dogma, Systematic Theology, Philosophy of Religion, Religion and Art, Religion and Music, Religion and Literature, Religion and Political Science, Religion and the Physical Sciences, Religion and the Natural Sciences, Religion and Public Policy, Religious Education — Elementary, Religious Education — Secondary, Religious Education — Post-Secondary
Types of publications: Essay/Lecture Collections, Reprints, General Interest Nonfiction — Adult, Fiction — Adult, Poetry, Scholarly Monographs, General Reference, Academic Reference
Books that incorporate a Reformed, Christian philosophical/theological perspective in their treatment of academic, social, cultural, and current issues.
In print: 17 titles.   1997: 2 titles.
ISBN Prefix(es): 0-932
Recent/Forthcoming Titles: Gerard Van Groningen, *Creation and Consummation*; John Van Dyk, *Letters to Lisa: Conversations with a Christian Teacher*; John H. Kok, *Patterns of the Western Mind*
No manuscript guidelines available
Preferred form of initial contact: Short written query
Send submissions to—
    James De Young
We accept few unsolicited submissions and none that do not clearly address the Reformed, Christian market.

47   Duke University Press
905 W Main St, Suite 18-B, Durham, NC 27701
Phone: 919-687-3600, 919-688-5134 (customer service)
Fax: 919-688-2615 (orders), 919-688-3524 (journals)
WWW homepage: www.duke.edu/web/dupress
Executive Director: Stanley Fish
Director of Publishing Operations: Stephen Cohn
Editor-in-Chief: Ken Wissoken

Subject areas: Religious Studies

Types of publications: Essay/Lecture Collections, General Interest Nonfiction — Adult, Translations, Scholarly Monographs

Duke University Press considers work on all the cultural—social, political, economic, and philosophic—aspects of religion. We do not ordinarily publish doctrinal works or theology.

In print: 25 titles.   1997: 7 titles.

ISBN Prefix(es): 0-8223

Recent/Forthcoming Titles: *In the Name of Elijah Muhammad: Louis Farrakhan and the Nation of Islam*; *Arguing Sainthood: Modernity, Psychoanalysis, and Islam*; *Between Jesus and the Market: The Emotions that Matter in Right-Wing America*

Manuscript guidelines free upon request

Preferred form of initial contact: Proposal package containing short written query, SASE, outline, 2 sample chapters, and author's C.V.

48   Eastern Orthodox Books

PO Box 302, Willits, CA 95490

Phone: 707-459-5424

Faith/denominational/cultural focus: Eastern Orthodox

Subject areas: Liturgy and Ritual, Prayer & Meditation, Missions, Spiritual Life/Personal Religion, Religious Biography, Doctrinal Theology & Dogma, Pastoral Theology, Pastoral Theology, Religious Education — Post-Secondary, Religious Education — Seminary

Types of publications: Devotional Guides, Liturgical Materials, Translations, Scholarly Monographs, Academic Reference

Most of our authors are dead. No, we didn't kill them; most are recognized as saints in the Eastern Orthodox Church. We are very strong in lives of the saints, Christian spirituality, Patristics, and specific Orthodox areas. Our books are strictly traditional Orthodox works, no innovations, theological dilution, or ecumenism. Theology doesn't change with passing fads or theories. Our primary goal is to provide works at the lowest possible price that will lead the reader to God and give him knowledge of His Church. While not a non-profit, we deliberately price our books to at best break even.

In print: 195 titles.   1997: 6 titles.

ISBN Prefix(es): 0-89981

No manuscript guidelines available.

Preferred form of initial contact: No unsolicited submissions accepted.

Limitations/Restrictions: We do not seek unsolicited original works, however we can use translators for some specific titles in our field (Greek, Russian, and Latin).

49   Eastern Press, Inc
PO Box 881, Bloomington, IN 47402
Publisher: Don Lee
Faith/denominational/cultural focus: Confucianism, Buddhism
Subject areas: Religious Life/Practice, Religious Thought/Theology, Religious Studies, Religion and Society, Sacred Literature, Religious Education
Eastern Press publishes works on Confucianism, Buddhism, and other Asiatic beliefs.
ISBN Prefix(es): 0-939758
Send #10 SASE for manuscript guidelines
Preferred form of initial contact: Proposal package containing SASE, cover letter, and outline (less than 5 pages).

50   The Edwin Mellen Press
415 Ridge St, PO Box 450, Lewiston, NY 14092-0450
Phone: 716-754-2266
Fax: 716-754-4056
E-mail: mellen@wzrd.com
Director: Herbert Richardson
Subject areas: Religious Life/Practice, Religious Thought/Theology, Religious Studies, Religion and Society, Sacred Literature, Religious Education
Types of publications: Scholarly Monographs, Dissertations, General Reference, Academic Reference
We publish in all academic disciplines, with a main market niche of research/university/seminary libraries and scholars. We have series subscriptions covering all facets of religion and philosophy.
Acquisitions focus for 1998-9: High-quality academic monographs for the university/seminary market.
In print: 1000 titles.   1997: 80 titles.

ISBN Prefix(es): 0-88946, 0-7734
Manuscript guidelines free upon request
Preferred form of initial contact: Proposal package containing short
    query and outline.
Send submissions to—
    All: John Rupnow, Acquisitions Director
    Biblical Press: Watson E. Mills, Acquisitions Editor

51   Wm B Eerdmans Publishing Co
255 Jefferson Ave SE, Grand Rapids, MI 49503-4570
Phone: 616-459-4591, 800-253-7521 (orders)
Fax: 616-459-6540
President: Wm. B. Eerdmans, Jr.
VP & Treasurer: Claire Vanderkam
VP & Ed.-in-Chief: Jon Pott
VP, Sales & Marketing: Samuel Eerdmans
Director, Sales: Theresa Peterlein
Publicist: Ina Vondiziano
Publicist: Anita Eerdmans
Customer Service Manager: Danford Gibbs
Rights & Permissions: Anne Salsich
Managing Editor: Charles Van Hof
Faith/denominational/cultural focus: Christian
Subject areas: Liturgy and Ritual, Prayer & Meditation, Religious
    Biography, Ethics, Systematic Theology, Pastoral Theology, History
    of Religion(s), Philosophy of Religion, Psychology of Religion,
    Religion and the Natural Sciences, Religion and Public Policy,
    Biblical Literature — Commentary & Hermeneutics, Koranic
    Literature — Commentary & Hermeneutics, Religious Education —
    Post-Secondary, Religious Education — Seminary
Types of publications: Classroom Instructional Materials (Textbooks),
    General Interest Nonfiction — Juvenile, Translations, Fiction —
    Juvenile, Scholarly Monographs, Academic Reference
Although Eerdmans publishes some regional books and other non-
    religious titles, it is essentially a religious publisher whose titles
    range from the academic to the semi-popular. It publishes some
    fiction and poetry, and is now publishing a growing number of books
    in the area of spirituality and the Christian life. It has long
    specialized in Biblical studies and theology and in religious

approaches to philosophy, history, art, literature, ethics, and contemporary social and cultural issues. Eerdmans also publishes a line of children's books which includes picture books and middle reader fiction and non-fiction.

Acquisitions focus for 1998-9: Theology & culture; biblical studies; ethics; religious history; spirituality and the Christian life; children's books.

In print: 900 titles.   1997: 140 titles.

ISBN Prefix(es): 0-8028

Recent/Forthcoming Titles: Marty & Marty, *The Promise of Winter*; Wolfhart Pannenberg, *New International Commentary on the New Testament — Philippians*; Nikki Grimes, *Come Sunday* (children's)

Manuscript guidelines free upon request

Preferred form of initial contact: Short written query or proposal package containing SASE, outline, 2 sample chapters and query letter.

Send submissions to—

Adult: Jon Pott, Editor-in-Chief

Children's: Amy De Vries, Director/Children's Books

52   Eisenbrauns

PO Box 275, Winona Lake, IN 46590

Phone: 219-269-2011

Fax: 219-269-6788

E-mail: orders@eisenbrauns.com

WWW homepage: www.eisenbrauns.com

Publisher: James E. Eisenbraun

Business Manager: David S. Terry

Chief Editor: Beverly B. Fields

Faith/denominational/cultural focus: Christian, Judaism

Subject areas: History of Religion(s), Sacred Languages, Religion and Classics, Anthropology of Religion, Religion and Archaeology, Biblical Literature — Commentary & Hermeneutics (Hebrew Bible/Old Testament), Biblical Literature — Philology & Linguistics (Hebrew Bible/Old, Biblical Literature — Cultural & Historical Contexts (Hebrew Bible/Old Testament), Biblical Literature — Translations (Hebrew Bible/Old Testament)

Types of publications: Illustrated Books, Reprints, Scholarly Monographs, Dissertations, General Reference, Language Reference, Academic Reference

Eisenbrauns specializes in academic monographs and language reference works focusing on Hebrew Bible/Old Testament, including archaeology and archaeological reports; we also publish on religions of ancillary areas, including Mesopotamia and Egypt.
In print: 80 titles.   1997: 13 titles.
  10% of titles author-subsidized
ISBN Prefix(es): 0-931464, 1-57506
Manuscript guidelines free upon request
Preferred form of initial contact: Short written query
Send submissions to—
    James E. Eisenbraun, Publisher
Limitations/Restrictions: We do not publish on modern religion.

53   Evangel Publishing House
Subsidiary/division of Brethren in Christ Board for Media Ministries
2000 Evangel Way, PO Box 189, Nappanee, IN 46550
Phone: 219-773-3164
Fax: 219-773-5934
E-mail: evangel.pubhouse@juno.com
Publisher: Roger L. Williams
Editor: Glen A. Pierce
Faith/denominational focus: Evangelical, Wesleyan, Anabaptist
Subject areas: Missions, Spiritual Life/Personal Religion, Religion and the Family, Ethics, Doctrinal Theology & Dogma, Systematic Theology, Pastoral Theology, Theological Education (methodology)
Types of publications: Classroom Instructional Materials, Reprints, General Interest Nonfiction — Adult, Academic Reference
In addition to publishing works specifically for the sponsoring denomination, Evangel Publishing House publishes books for use by colleges and seminaries, as well as by pastors, teachers, and lay persons in congregations. Evangel Publishing House books are faithful to the Biblical witness of historical Christianity while addressing issues and questions faced by today's increasingly postmodern culture.
Acquisitions focus for 1998-9: Academic titles for use in Christian colleges, seminaries, and divinity schools.
In print: 30 titles.   1997: 10 titles.
  10% of titles author-subsidized

Recent/Forthcoming Titles: Don Thorson, *Theological Resources for Ministry*; Barry Callan, *Faithful in the Meantime*; David Thompson, *Bible Study That Works*
No manuscript guidelines available
Preferred form of initial contact: Short written query
Send submissions to—
    Glen A. Pierce, Editor

54   Exploration Press of the Chicago Theological Seminary
5757 University Ave, Chicago, IL 60637
Phone: 773-752-5757
Co-Editor: Perry LeFevre
Co-Editor: W. Widick Schroeder
Subject areas: Religious Life/Practice, Religious Thought/Theology, Interdisciplinary Studies, Religious Education
Types of publications: Classroom Instructional Materials, Essay/Lecture Collections, Reprints, Scholarly Monographs, Academic Reference
In print: 29 titles.   1997: 1 title.
ISBN Prefix(es): 0-913552
No manuscript guidelines available
No unsolicited submissions accepted

55   Faith & Life Press
Subsidiary/division of General Conference Mennonite Church
718 Main St, PO Box 347, Newton, KS 67114
Phone: 316-283-5100
Fax: 316-283-0454
E-mail: flp@gcmc.org
WWW homepage: www2.southwind.net/~gcmc
Director of Operations: Dennis Good
Director of Customer Service: Christopher Scott
Editorial Director: Byron Rempel-Burkholder
Faith/denominational/cultural focus: General Conference Mennonite Church, Anabaptist, and interdenominational Christian
Subject areas: Prayer & Meditation, Spiritual Life/Personal Religion, Religion and the Family, Theological Education (methodology), Religion and Art, Religion and Music, Religion and Gender Studies,

Methodologies of Study and Teaching, Religion in Popular Culture/Media, Religious Education — Theory and Methodology, Religious Education — Elementary, Religious Education — Secondary, Religious Education — Post-Secondary, Religious Education — Adult

Types of publications: Music, Devotional Guides, Liturgical Materials, Sunday School Curriculum, Thematic Elective Studies (adults)

Faith & Life Press focuses its publishing efforts on products for use by groups and individuals within congregations. Our primary audience is the Mennonite community; our secondary audience includes people in the broader Christian community. Faith & Life Press supports this editorial focus by publishing products for all ages in these three categories: 1) Christian Education Resources; 2) Bible Studies and Electives; and 3) Spirituality and Worship Resources. Faith & Life Press publishes systematic curriculum series for use in Sunday school and other Christian education settings. We are also involved in publishing periodicals for personal reading as well as for resourcing volunteers in the congregation, and individual titles in these product categories.

Acquisitions focus for 1998-9: Due to transitions in acquisitions staff, this has not been finalized; however, one focus will likely be parenting resources.

In print: 130 titles.   1997: 15 titles.

ISBN Prefix(es): 0-87303

Recent/Forthcoming Titles: *Faith for the Journey: Youth Explore the Confession of Faith*; *Living the Vision: Leadership and Community*; *Kids and Values* (VBS curriculum)

Manuscript guidelines free upon request

Preferred form of initial contact: Short written query

Send submissions to—

    Youth, adult & congregational resources:
      Byron Rempel-Burkholder, Editorial Director
    Children's resources: Elizabeth Pankratz, Children's Editor

56   Fortress Press
Imprint of Augsburg Fortress Publishers
PO Box 1209, Minneapolis, MN 55440
Phone: 612-330-3433
Fax: 612-330-3215
WWW homepage: www.elca.org/afp/afphome.html
Editorial Director: Dr. Henry F. French
Senior Editor: J. Michael West
Faith/denominational/cultural focus: Interfaith, Ecumenical
Subject areas: Liturgy and Ritual, Prayer & Meditation, Vocational/Pastoral Guidance, Preaching & Homiletics, Ethics, Doctrinal Theology & Dogma, Systematic Theology, Pastoral Theology, Contextual Theologies, Religion and Cultural/Ethnic Studies, Religion and Gender Studies, Biblical Literature — Cultural & Historical Contexts, Talmudic Literature — Cultural & Historical Contexts, Religious Education — Seminary
Types of publications: Classroom Instructional Materials, Liturgical Materials, Scholarly Monographs, General Reference, Academic Reference
Fortress Press is an imprint Augsburg Fortress Publishers, publishing house of the Evangelical Lutheran Church of America. It is academic, ecumenical, international, and inclusive in its scope. Its chief areas of publishing are Hebrew Bible, New Testament, history of Christianity, theology, ethics, and resources for professionals in ministry. Its chief readerships are scholars and professors; college, university and seminary students; professionals in ministry; and the general public. The press sponsors many series, including Hermeneia, Overtures to Biblical Theology, Guides to Theological Inquiry, and Theology and the Sciences.
In print: 550 titles.   1997: 34 titles.
ISBN Prefix(es): 0-8006
Recent/Forthcoming Titles: Rosemary Radford Ruether, *Women and Redemption*; Luke Timothy Johnson, *Religious Experience in Earliest Christianity*; Walter Brueggemann, *Theology of the Old Testament*
Manuscript guidelines free upon request
Preferred form of initial contact: Proposal package containing SASE, outline, 1-2 sample chapters, author's C.V., and information on page length, completion schedule, and competition.
Please allow 60-90 days for manuscript review.

57   Forward Movement Publications
412 Sycamore Street, Cincinnati, OH 45202
Phone: 513-721-6659
Fax: 513-421-0315
E-mail: forward.movement@ecunet.org
WWW homepage: dfms.org/fmp
Associate Director: Sally B. Sedgwick
Business Manager: Jane Paraskevopoulos
Faith/denominational/cultural focus: Episcopalian, Christian
Subject areas: Prayer & Meditation, Spiritual Life/Personal Religion,
    Religion and the Family
Types of publications: Essay/Lecture Collections, Devotional Guides,
    General Interest Nonfiction — Adult, Self-Help
Forward Movement is committed to publishing small (usually) low cost,
    high quality books and pamphlets to assist individuals in their life
    and ministry.
Acquisitions focus for 1998-9: Middle school fiction (ages 8-12) and
    science fiction exploring theological and Christian themes.
In print: 400 titles.   1997: 32 titles.
ISBN Prefix(es): 0-88028
Recent/Forthcoming Titles: *Building Up the Church*; *400 Years:
    Anglican/Episcopal Mission among American Indians*
Send #10 SASE for manuscript guidelines
Preferred form of initial contact: Proposal package containing at least 2
    chapters (or complete manuscript).
Send submissions to—
    Adult: Edward S. Gleason, Editor & Director
    Children/youth: Mary Barwell, Assistant Editor

58   Foundation for *A Course in Miracles*
1275 Tennanah Lake Rd, Roscoe, NY 12776
Phone: 607-498-4116
Fax: 607-498-5325
WWW homepage: facim.org
Subject areas: Spiritual Life/Personal Religion, *A Course in Miracles*,
    Philosophy of Religion, Psychology of Religion
The Foundation publishes books, audio, and video tapes on *A Course in
    Miracles* to help students of the Course with their understanding of

its principles and the application of those principles to their everyday lives.

In print: 69 titles.   1997: 1 title.

ISBN Prefix(es): 0-933291

Recent/Forthcoming Titles: *The Message of* A Course in Miracles, *vol. 1: All Are Called; The Message of* A Course in Miracles, *vol. 2: Few Choose to Listen*

No manuscript guidelines available

No unsolicited submissions accepted

59   The Free Press

Subsidiary/division of Simon & Schuster

1230 6th Ave, New York, NY 10020

Faith/denominational/cultural focus: Judaica

Subject areas: Ethics, Comparative Religions, History of Religion(s), Philosophy of Religion, Religion and Cultural/Ethnic Studies, Religion and Gender Studies, Psychology of Religion, Sociology of Religion, Anthropology of Religion, Religion in Popular Culture/Media, Religion and Law, Religion and Public Policy especially

Types of publications: General Interest Nonfiction — Adult

ISBN Prefix(es): 0-684

No manuscript guidelines available

Preferred form of initial contact: Proposal package containing SASE.

60   Genesis Publishing Co, Inc

1547 Great Pond Rd, North Andover, MA 01845-1216

Phone: 508-688-6688

Fax: 508-688-8686

E-mail: genesisbooks@compuserve.com

WWW homepage: ourworld.compuserve.com/homepages/genesisbooks

Publicity: Trudy Doucette

Subject areas: Spiritual Life/Personal Religion, Doctrinal Theology & Dogma, Systematic Theology, Natural Theology, Philosophy of Religion, Religion and the Physical Sciences, Religion and the Natural Sciences, Religious Ed. — Seminary, Religious Ed. — Adult

Types of publications: Gen'l Interest Nonfiction and Fiction — Adult
Genesis Publishing carries trade books on science/philosophy/religion.
In print: 9 titles. 1997: 3 titles.   ISBN Prefix(es): 1-886670
No manuscript guidelines available
Preferred form of initial contact: Proposal package containing SASE,
    outline, and 1 sample chapter.
Send submissions to—
    Gerard Vershuuren, President

61   Georgetown University Press
3619 'O' Street NW, Washington, DC 20007
Orders: PO Box 4866, Hampden Station, Baltimore, MD 21211
Phone: 202-687-5889, 410-516-6995 (orders)
Fax: 202-687-6340, 410-516-6998 (orders)
Faith/denominational/cultural focus: Roman Catholic
Subject areas: Ethics, Pastoral Theology, Religion and Political Science,
    Religion and Public Policy
Types of publications: Classroom Instructional Materials,
    Essay/Lecture Collections, Scholarly Monographs, Academic
    Reference
Georgetown University Press publishes books in ethics, bioethics,
    Christian ethics, ethics and education, ethics and the professions,
    Jesuit studies, and theology. The Press' goal is to further the
    University's mission of scholarly research by making current work in
    these fields available to scholars and the general public.
In print: 75 titles.   1997: 7 titles.
ISBN Prefix(es): 0-87840
Recent/Forthcoming Titles: *Choosing Life: A Dialogue on* Evangelium
    Vitae; *Fragmentation and Consensus: Communitarian and Casuist
    Bioethics; Virtue Ethics: A Critical Reader*
No manuscript guidelines available
Preferred form of initial contact: Proposal package containing SASE,
    outline, 1-3 sample chapters, author résumé or C.V.
Send submissions to—
    John Samples, Ph.D., Director
Submissions to the series "Moral Traditions and Moral Arguments"
    should be sent to editor James F. Keenan, S.J., Weston School of
    Theology, 3 Phillips Place, Cambridge, MA 02138

62   The K S Giniger Company, Inc
250 W 57th Street, New York, NY 10107

Phone: 212-570-7499

Fax: 212-369-6692

President: Kenneth Seeman Giniger

U.K. Representative: Mariella Wolf

European Representative: Jeanne-Marie Herter

Subject areas: Prayer & Meditation, Spiritual Life/Personal Religion, Religion and Health, History of Religion(s), Religion and the Physical Sciences, Religion and the Natural Sciences

Types of publications: Devotional Guides, General Interest Nonfiction — Adult, Self-Help, General Reference

Our general non-fiction list includes daily devotionals and books of inspiration and self-help. We do not "acquire"; we commission books for which we see a market. All our titles are co-published in association with other publishers.

In print: 24 titles.   1997: 2 titles.

Recent/Forthcoming Titles: *Daily Word*; *Life Beyond Death*; *Prayers and Devotions from Pope John Paul II*

No manuscript guidelines available

No unsolicited submissions accepted

63   Gordon Press
PO Box 459, Bowling Green Station, New York, NY 10004

Subject areas: Liturgy and Ritual, Prayer & Meditation, Spiritual Life/Personal Religion, Religion and Health, Ethics, Doctrinal Theology & Dogma, Natural Theology, Comparative Religions, History of Religion(s), Folklore, Sacred Languages, Religion and Literature, Psychology of Religion, Sociology of Religion, Anthropology of Religion, Religion and Archaeology, Religion and Economics, Religion and Political Science, Religion and the Natural Sciences, Religion in Popular Culture/Media, Biblical Literature — Cultural & Historical Contexts, Talmudic Literature — Cultural & Historical Contexts, Koranic Literature — Cultural & Historical Contexts, Buddhist Literature — Cultural & Historical Contexts

Types of publications: Translations, Self-Help, Scholarly Monographs, Dissertations, General, Language, and Academic Reference

We are attempting to explore areas heretofore not adequately covered in various aspects of religious history.

Acquisitions focus for 1998-9: Scholarly works on origins of Judaism, Christianity, Islam, and Buddhism.

In print: 128 titles.   1997: 14 titles.

Recent/Forthcoming Titles: *Martin Buber: A Critical Anthology; Origins of Medieval Jewry; Jesus as a Jew*

Send SASE w/$4 postage for MS guidelines.

Preferred form of initial contact: Proposal package containing short written query and SASE.

Send submissions to—
    Sol Gordon, President

64   Hachai Publishing
156 Chester Ave, Brooklyn, NY 11218
Phone: 718-633-0100
Fax: 718-633-0103
Faith/denominational/cultural focus: Judaism
Subject areas: Religious Education — Elementary
Types of publications: Illustrated Books, General Interest Nonfiction — Juvenile, Fiction — Juvenile

Children's books play a vital role in every Jewish home, classroom, and library. Hachai Publishing is dedicated to producing high-quality children's literature with Jewish themes. Our books promote universal values—such as doing good deeds, sharing, kindness, and charity—and teach Jewish history and tradition. The work of exciting new authors and artists create books that parents and their children will enjoy over and over again.

Acquisitions focus for 1998-9: Books that address new ways for children to take an active role in performing good deeds, celebrating holidays, and taking pride in their rich Jewish heritage.

In print: 3 titles. 1997: 1 title.   ISBN Prefix(es): 0-922613

Recent/Forthcoming Titles: *The Wise Little Judge and Other Stories; The Three Gifts and Other Stories; Nine Spoons: A Chanuka Story*

Send #10 SASE for manuscript guidelines

Preferred form of initial contact: Proposal package containing SASE; short preschool books should be sent in entirety.

Send submissions to—
    D. L. Rosenfeld, Submissions Editor

Limitations/Restrictions: Not looking for comparative religion. Authors need genuine knowledge of Jewish experience, holidays, and traditions.

65   Halo Books, LLC
112 Oak Ave, Novato, CA 94945
Phone: 415-892-0649
Fax: 415-434-3441
Subject areas: Spiritual Life/Personal Religion, Psychology of Religion
Types of publications: Self-Help
Our titles focus on inspirational, personal growth, and psychological genres.
In print: 6 titles.
ISBN Prefix(es): 1-879904, 0-9622874
No manuscript guidelines available
Preferred form of initial contact: Proposal package containing SASE, outline, and sample chapters.

66   HarperSanFrancisco
Subsidiary/division of HarperCollins Publishers
353 Sacramento Street, Suite 500, San Francisco, CA 94111-3653
Phone: 415-477-4400
Fax: 415-477-4444
E-mail: hcsanfrancisco@harpercollins.com
WWW homepage: www.harpercollins.com/sanfran
Publishing Director: R. Diane Gedymin
Subject areas: Prayer & Meditation, Vocational/Pastoral Guidance, Preaching & Homiletics, Spiritual Life/Personal Religion, Religion and the Family, Religion and Health, Doctrinal Theology & Dogma, Comparative Religions, History of Religion(s), Mythology, Sacred Languages, Philosophy of Religion, Religion and Gender Studies, Psychology of Religion, Religion in Popular Culture/Media, Sacred Literature — Translations
Types of publications: General Interest Nonfiction — Adult, Translations, Self-Help, General Reference, Academic Reference
HarperSanFrancisco is dedicated to publishing books of the highest quality that illuminate diverse religious traditions and spiritual journeys and that offer paths toward personal growth and holistic well-being.
In print: 700 titles.   1997: 48 titles.
ISBN Prefix(es): 0-06

Recent/Forthcoming Titles: Billy Graham, *Just As I Am* ; Robert Funk &
The Jesus Seminar, *The Acts of Jesus*; Robert A. Johnson & Jerry M.
Ruhl, *Balancing Heaven and Earth*
No manuscript guidelines available
Preferred form of initial contact: No unsolicited submissions accepted;
agented submissions only.
Send submissions to—
Mark Chimsky, Editorial Director

67   Harvard University Press
79 Garden St, Cambridge, MA 02138
Phone: 617-495-2600
Fax: 617-496-4677
WWW homepage: www.hup.harvard.edu
Director: William P. Sisler
Subject areas: Comparative Religions, History of Religion(s),
Mythology, Interdisciplinary Studies, Religion and Society, Sacred
Literature — Cultural & Historical Contexts
Types of publications: Scholarly Monographs, General Reference,
Academic Reference
1997: 15 titles.
ISBN Prefix(es): 674-
Recent/Forthcoming Titles: James Kugel, *The Bible As It Was*; Mark
Chaves, *Ordaining Women*; Fritz Graf, *Magic in the Ancient World*
No manuscript guidelines available.
Preferred form of initial contact: Proposal package containing outline,
and 1-2 sample chapters.
Send submissions to—
Margaretta Fulton, Gen'l Editor for Humanities

68   Hendrickson Publishers Inc
140 Summit St, PO Box 3473, Peabody, MA 01960
Phone: 508-532-6546, 800-358-3111 (sales and orders)
Fax: 508-531-8146
E-mail: editorial@hendrickson.com
President: Stephen J. Hendrickson
VP Marketing: David L. Townsley

Faith/denominational/cultural focus: Interdenominational, interfaith publishing within the Judeo-Christian traditions

Subject areas: Preaching & Homiletics, Spiritual Life/Personal Religion, Pastoral Theology, Religion and Classics, Religion and Archaeology, Biblical Literature — Commentary & Hermeneutics, Biblical Literature — Philology & Linguistics, Biblical Literature — Cultural & Historical Contexts, Biblical Literature — Translations, Religious Education — Seminary

Types of publications: Essay/Lecture Collections, Reprints, Translations, Scholarly Monographs, Dissertations, Language Reference, Academic Reference

Hendrickson Publishers' program focuses on religious studies within the Judeo-Christian tradition, publishing especially in four areas: 1) language reference, including Greek and Latin lexical and grammatical aids; 2) texts (including translations) designed for introductory and upper-level Biblical history courses, ancient Near Eastern studies, Hebrew Bible, New Testament exegesis, archaeology, world of the Bible, early Christian studies, and church history into the 20th Century; 3) pastoral topics, including preaching, prayer, spirituality, healing, and theology; 4) classic reprints, such as the apostolic fathers, language reference works, the writings of Josephus and Philo, and a 38 vol. collection of the writings of the church fathers.

Acquisitions focus for 1998-9: Israelite history, Dead Sea Scrolls, language reference, translations, Second Temple Judaism, NT theology, Pauline Christianity, spirituality, and church history.

In print: 200 titles.   1997: 30 titles.

ISBN Prefix(es): 0-913573, 0-917006, 0-943575, 1-56563

Recent/Forthcoming Titles: E. Jenni & C. Westermann, *Theological Lexicon of the Old Testament*; J. Gnilka, *Jesus of Nazareth: Message and History*; Niels Peter Lemeche, *Prelude to Israel's Past: Background and Beginning of Israelite History and Identity*

Manuscript guidelines free upon request.

Preferred form of initial contact: Proposal package containing SASE, outline, 2 sample chapters, and author's C.V.

54

69   Humanics Publishing Group
Subsidiary/division of Humanics Limited
Imprint of Quality Paperbacks
1482 Mecaslin St, NW, Atlanta, GA 30809
Phone: 404-874-2176
Fax: 404-874-1976
E-mail: trade@humanicspub.com
Chairman: Gary Wilson
Faith/denominational/cultural focus: Taoism, Buddhism, Zen, Sufi, Ching, Confucian
Subject areas: Prayer & Meditation, Spiritual Life/Personal Religion, Religion and Health, Religious Biography, Ethics, Natural Theology, Comparative Religions, History of Religion(s), Mythology, Folklore, Philosophy of Religion, Religion and Art, Religion and Literature, Religion and Cultural/Ethnic Studies, Religion and Gender Studies, Psychology of Religion, Sociology of Religion, Religion and Economics, Koranic Literature — Commentary & Hermeneutics, Koranic Literature — Cultural & Historical Contexts, Koranic Literature — Translations, Tantric/Vedic Lit. — Commentary & Hermeneutics, Tantric/Vedic Lit. — Cultural & Historical Contexts, Tantric/Vedic Lit. — Translations, Buddhist Literature — Commentary & Hermeneutics, Buddhist Literature — Cultural & Historical Contexts, Buddhist Literature — Translations, Confucian Literature — Commentary & Hermeneutics, Confucian Literature — Cultural & Historical Contexts, Confucian Literature — Translations, Taoist Literature — Commentary & Hermeneutics, Taoist Literature — Cultural & Historical Contexts, Taoist Literature — Translations
Types of publications: Classroom Instructional Materials, Illustrated Books, Translations, Self-Help, Poetry, Scholarly Monographs, Childcare
Guides to self-transformation, often reached through eastern religions/philosophies.
Acquisitions focus for 1998-9: Taoism, Confucian, Zen, any Mysticism.
In print: 200 titles.   1997: 8 titles.   ISBN Prefix(es): 0-89334
Recent/Forthcoming Titles: *Creative Tao*; *Way of Virtue*; *Tao of Design*
Send SASE for manuscript guidelines
Preferred form of initial contact: Short written query or proposal package containing SASE and outline
Send submissions to—
    W. Arthur Bligh

70   Ide House
Subsidiary/division of Publishers Associates
PO Box 140361, Irving, TX 75104-0361
Mailing: 4631 Harvey Drive, Mesquite, TX 75150-1609
Phone: 972-681-9190
E-mail: idehouse.com
WWW homepage: www.idehouse.com
CIO: John M. Smith
Subject areas: History of Religion(s), Mythology, Religion and Classics, Sacred Literature — Commentary & Hermeneutics, Sacred Literature — Philology & Linguistics, Sacred Literature — Cultural & Historical Contexts, Sacred Literature — Translations
Types of publications: Scholarly Monographs, Dissertations
Ide House's religion-related list focuses on progressive/liberal titles that are gender-neutral, feminist, and devoted to social involvement.
In print: 100 titles.   1997: 5 titles.
ISBN Prefix(es): 0-86663
Send #10 SASE for manuscript guidelines
Preferred form of initial contact: Short written query with postcard only for reply.
Send submissions to—
    General Works: Art James, Facilitator
    Women-oriented works: Dr. Mary Markal, Sr. VP. MS Committee
Limitations/Restrictions: All manuscripts must be fully documented: notes and bibliography; we emphasize primary sources.

71   Indiana University Press
601 North Morton St, Bloomington, IN 47404-3797
E-mail Orders: iuporder@indiana.edu
Phone: 812-855-4203, 800-842-6796 (customer service)
Fax: 812-855-8507
E-mail: iupress@indiana.edu
WWW homepage: www.indiana.edu/~iupress
Director: John Gallman
Marketing Manager: Susan Harlish
Sales Manager: Richard Granich
Managing Editor: Jeff Ankrom
Managing Editor: Jeffrey Ankrom

Subject areas: Comparative Religions, History of Religion(s), Mythology, Folklore, Philosophy of Religion, Religion and Cultural/Ethnic Studies, Religion and Gender Studies, Anthropology of Religion, Religion and the Physical Sciences, Religion and the Natural Sciences, Religion in Popular Culture/Media, Religion and Public Policy

Types of publications: Classroom Instructional Materials, General Interest Nonfiction — Adult, Scholarly Monographs, Academic Reference

Our program focuses on the academic study of religion, chiefly in the United States, including Native America, and also as it involves our area studies programs: the Middle East, Africa, the Caribbean and Central America, and Eastern Europe. We seek manuscripts that are interdisciplinary and incorporate new methodologies that focus on the meaning and power of religious movements as religion, on ritual, on the culture (including material culture of religion), on the philosophy of religion, on women and religion, and on contemporary events and issues in religion. We are interested in books that present current scholarship in a form accessible to the general reader.

Acquisitions focus for 1998-9: Books for the widest possible audience in areas such as lived religion, material culture of religion, ritual, women and religion, spirituality movements, and the like; also interested in classroom supplemental texts and major scholarly reference projects.

In print: 115 titles.   1997: 12 titles.

ISBN Prefix(es): 0-253

Recent/Forthcoming Titles: Richard B. Turner, *Islam and the African American Experience*; Bret E. Carroll, *Spiritualism in Antebellum America*; Kay Almere Reid, *Time and Sacrifice in the Aztec Cosmos*

Manuscript guidelines free upon request

Preferred form of initial contact: Short written query or proposal package containing SASE, outline, 2 sample chapters, and author's C.V.

Send submissions to—

    All subjects except philosophy of religion and Jewish Studies:
        Robert J. Sloan, Sponsoring Editor

    Philosophy of religion and Jewish studies: Janet Rabinowitch, Senior Sponsoring Editor

72   Innisfree Press (formerly LuraMedia)
136 Roumfort Road, Philadelphia, PA 19119-1632
Phone: 215-247-4085
Fax: 215-247-2343
E-mail: InnisfreeP@aol.com
Subject areas: Prayer & Meditation, Spiritual Life/Personal Religion
Types of publications: General Interest Nonfiction — Adult, Self-Help
Innisfree Press was founded in 1996 to acquire and continue the best of
    spiritual, psychology/self-help, and women's studies books from
    LuraMedia. Our mission is to publish books that nourish the spiritual
    journey, stimulate original thinking, and invite creative responses.
Acquisitions focus for 1998-9: Books that bring spirituality into the
    everyday world: into work (*The Job Hunter's Spiritual Companion*);
    into the family (*No Kin Like Kindred Spirits*); and into personal
    growth (*A Return to the Sea*)
In print: 18 titles.   1997: 5 titles.
ISBN Prefix(es): 0-931055, 1-880913
Recent/Forthcoming Titles: *Spiritual Lemons: Biblical Women,
    Righteous Rage and Irreverent Laughter; Tracks in the Straw: Tales
    Spun from the Manger; Sabbath Sense: A Spiritual Antidote for the
    Overworked*
Manuscript guidelines free upon request
Preferred form of initial contact: Proposal package containing SASE,
    outline, 1 sample chapter, comparison to potential competition and
    identification of what makes the work unique, and author's
    credentials.
Send submissions to—
Marcia Broucek, Editor-in-Chief
Limitations/Restrictions: No novels, poetry, or children's books; adult
    nonfiction only.

73   Institute of Jesuit Sources
3700 W Pine Blvd, St. Louis, MO 63108
Phone: 314-977-7257
Fax: 314-977-7263
Director: John W. Padberg, SJ
Faith/denominational/cultural focus: Roman Catholic (Society of Jesus)
Subject areas: Prayer & Meditation, Spiritual Life/Personal Religion,
    Religious Biography, Spiritual Theology, History of Religion(s),

Biblical Literature — Cultural & Historical Contexts, Biblical Literature — Translations

Types of publications: Classroom Instructional Materials, Reprints, Devotional Guides, General Interest Nonfiction — Adult, Translations, Scholarly Monographs, Academic Reference

The Institute publishes works bearing on the origins, history, and spirituality of the Society of Jesus (Jesuits) in several categories or series: 1) Jesuit primary sources in English translation; 2) modern scholarly studies of the Jesuits in English translation; 3) original studies composed in English; 4) studies on Jesuit topics; and 5) prayer.

In print: 67 titles.

ISBN Prefix(es): 0-912422, 1-880810

Recent/Forthcoming Titles: *Terpsichore at Louis-le-Grand: Baroque Dance in the Jesuit Stage in Paris*; *Tibet: The Jesuit Century*; *The Spiritual Writings of Pierre Favre*

No manuscript guidelines available.

Preferred form of initial contact: Short written query.

Limitations/Restrictions: The material submitted must be concerned with the history and/or spirituality of the Society of Jesus.

74   International Awakening Press

Subsidiary/division of International Awakening Ministries

PO Box 232, Wheaton, IL 60189

Street: 123-145 North Washington, Wheaton, IL 60189

Phone: 630-653-8616

Fax: 630-653-8616

E-mail: Internationalawakening@juno.com

Editor: Richard Owen Roberts

Sales: Robert Owen Roberts

Accounting: Margaret J. Roberts

Faith/denominational/cultural focus: Inter-denominational Christian

Subject areas: Preaching & Homiletics, Missions, Spiritual Life/Personal Religion, Religious Biography, Doctrinal Theology & Dogma, Systematic Theology, Pastoral Theology, History of Religion(s), Biblical Literature — Commentary & Hermeneutics

Types of publications: Books-on-Tape, Scholarly Monographs, Dissertations, Academic Reference

We specialize in publications pertaining to revival and reformation including biographies, histories, lectures, sermons and treatises dealing with the awakening of the church throughout the world.
In print: 22 titles.   1997: 3 titles.
ISBN Prefix(es): 0-926474
Recent/Forthcoming Titles: *The Turn of the Tide; Show Me Thy Glory; Twenty-Four Questions to Ask in the Face of Apparent Revival*
No manuscript guidelines available
Preferred form of initial contact: Short written query
Send submissions to—
      Richard Owen Roberts, Editor
Limitations/Restrictions: Scholarly material only.

75   International Religious Foundation
Subsidiary/division of Paragon House
4 West 43rd St, New York, NY 10036
Phone: 212-869-6023
Fax: 212-869-6424
Faith/denominational/cultural focus: Interfaith
Subject areas: Religious Thought/Theology, Comparative Religions, Interdisciplinary Studies, Religion and Society
Types of publications: Classroom Instructional Materials, Essay & Lecture Collections, Scholarly Monographs
We publish books that promote greater inter-religious understanding and cooperation and which illuminate religion's contribution to social transformation.
In print: 50 titles.   1997: 15 titles.
5% of titles author-subsidized
Recent/Forthcoming Titles: *Religion and the Ideal; Christian-Muslim Dialogue; Religion in Africa*
No manuscript guidelines available
Preferred form of initial contact: Proposal package containing SASE, outline, and sample chapters.
Send submissions to—
      Thomas G. Walsh, Editor

76   International Scholars Publishing

7831 Woodmont Ave, #345, Bethesda, MD 20814
Phone: 301-654-7417
Fax: 301-654-7336
E-mail: austinisp1@aol.com
CEO: Dr. Robert West
Editorial Director: Dr. Andrew Woznicki
Subject areas: Liturgy and Ritual, Missions, Religious Biography, Ethics, Process Theology, Systematic Theology, Natural Theology, Theological Education (Methodology), Religious Studies, Religion and Society, Biblical Literature — Commentary & Hermeneutics, Religious Education — Public policy/Legal Issues, Religious Education — Seminary
Types of publications: Reprints, Translations, Academic Reference
Through its imprints Catholics Scholars Press and Christian Universities Press, ISP has a strong interest in theology and the study of religion with special emphasis on revised dissertations (the Distinguished Research series) and independent monographs.
Acquisitions focus for 1998-9: Special interest in Africa and African theology and practice; also religion and the law and Biblical studies.
In print: 124 titles.   1997: 61 title.
ISBN Prefix(es): 1-883255, 1-57309
Recent/Forthcoming Titles: Adamo, *Africa and Africans in the Old Testament*; Peters, *A Gadamerian Reading of the Theology of Rahmer*; Weikart, *The Myth of Dietrich Bonhoffer*
Manuscript guidelines free upon request
Preferred form of initial contact: Proposal package containing SASE, outline, and 2 sample chapters.
Send submissions to—
    Catholic theology: Dr. Andrew Woznicki, Editorial Director
    Religious studies/Africa: Dr. Robert West, CEO
    Evangelical/History: Dr. Calvin Janssen, Editor
Please estimate timetable and printed page count when submitting; we expect camera-ready material from our contracted authors.

77   International Students, Inc

PO Box C, Colorado Springs, CO 80901
Street Address: 2864 S Circle Drive, #600, Colorado Springs, CO 80906
Phone: 719-576-2700
Fax: 719-576-5363
E-mail: kmaas@isionline.org
WWW homepage: www.isionline.org
President/CEO: Tom Phillips
Faith/denominational/cultural focus: Christian (int'l student ministry)
Subject areas: Comparative Religions
Types of publications: Classroom Instructional Materials, Self-Help
We publish materials uniquely designed for ministry to international
    students. Much is Bible study material appropriate to internationals.
    We also do a number of pieces that are designed to train American
    volunteers to do international student ministry, particularly pieces
    on cross-cultural sensitivity and comparative religions.
Acquisitions focus for 1998-9: Limited to the areas noted above with
    international student ministry as the unique focus.
In print: 10 titles.
No manuscript guidelines available
Preferred form of initial contact: Short written query
Send submissions to—
    Kathy Maas, VP, Production/Communications
Limitations/Restrictions: We primarily publish short booklets.

78   InterVarsity Press

Subsidiary/division of InterVarsity Christian Fellowship/USA
PO Box 1400, Downers Grove, IL 60515
Street Address: 430 E Plaza Drive, Westmont, IL 60559
Phone: 630-887-2500, 603-887-2510 (Voice Mail)
Fax: 630-887-2520
E-mail: mail@ivpress.com
WWW homepage: www.ivpress.com
Executive Director: Robert A. Fryling
Editorial Director: Andrew T. LePeau
Dir. Sales & Marketing: Don Stephenson
Business Manager: Jim Hagen
Prod. & Fulfillment Manager: Nancy Fox
Faith/denominational/cultural focus: Christian

Subject areas: Prayer & Meditation, Vocational/Pastoral Guidance, Preaching & Homiletics, Missions, Spiritual Life/Personal Religion, Religion and the Family, Religion and Health, Religious Biography, Ethics, Doctrinal Theology & Dogma, Process Theology, Systematic Theology, Pastoral Theology, Theological Education (methodology), Comparative Religions, History of Religion(s), Philosophy of Religion, Religion and Art, Religion and Music, Religion and Literature, Religion and Cultural/Ethnic Studies, Religion and Gender Studies, Psychology of Religion, Sociology of Religion, Religion and Economics, Religion and Political Science, Religion and the Physical Sciences, Religion and the Natural Sciences, Religion in Popular Culture/Media, Religion and Law, Biblical Literature — Commentary & Hermeneutics, Biblical Literature — Cultural & Historical Contexts, Religious Ed. — Theory and Methodology

Types of publications: Illustrated Books, Essay/Lecture Collections, Self-Help, Fiction — Juvenile, Scholarly Monographs, General Reference, Academic Reference

InterVarsity Press is the book publishing division of InterVarsity Christian Fellowship of the USA. Manuscripts must be Biblically-based and reflect mature understanding. We publish in four main areas: academic, reference, Bible study, and general. IVP is broadly evangelical in its outlook, willing to consider appropriate manuscripts from Protestant, Catholic, and Orthodox authors.

Acquisitions focus for 1998-9: IVP seeks both core and supplementary texts as well as ground-breaking academic studies. IVP also seeks books for and about small groups, reference works, and books for a general lay audience dealing with contemporary issues or spiritual/faith development.

In print: 720 titles.   1997: 75 titles.

ISBN Prefix(es): 0-8308, 0-87784

Recent/Forthcoming Titles: Joyce Huggett, *Praying the Parables*; Gregory A. Boyd, *God at War*; Ralph Martin and Peter Davids, eds., *Dictionary of the Later New Testament and Its Developments*

Manuscript guidelines free upon request

Preferred form of initial contact: Proposal package containing SASE, outline, 2 sample chapters, and author's resume or C.V.

Send submissions to—

Academic & General: Rodney Clapp, Senior Editor

Reference & Academic: Dan Reid, Senior Editor

Academic: Jim Hoover, Senior Editor

Bible Study & General: Cindy Bunch-Hotaling, Associate Editor

79   Jewish Lights Publishing
Subsidiary/division of Longhill Partners Inc
Sunset Farm Offices, Rte 4, PO Box 237, Woodstock, VT 05091
Phone: 802-457-4000
Fax: 802-457-4004
E-mail: editorial@jewishlights.com
WWW homepage: www.jewishlights.com
Faith/denominational/cultural focus: Judaism (wisdom tradition)
Subject areas: Liturgy and Ritual, Prayer & Meditation, Spiritual
    Life/Personal Religion, Religion and the Family, Religion and Health
Types of publications: Classroom Instructional Materials, Illustrated
    Books, Reprints, General Interest Nonfiction — Adult, General
    Interest Nonfiction — Juvenile, Self-Help, General Reference
Jewish Lights publishes for people of all faiths and all backgrounds who
    yearn for books that attract, engage, educate, and spiritually inspire.
    Our authors are at the forefront of spiritual thought and deal with
    the quest for self and for meaning in life by drawing on the Jewish
    wisdom tradition. Our books cover topics including history,
    spirituality, life cycle, children's, self-help, recovery, theology and
    philosophy. We do not publish autobiography, biography, or fiction.
Acquisitions focus for 1998-9: Explaining Judaism for Christians and
    Muslims; explaining Christianity and Islam for Jews. Text studies
    (as part of daily life—not exclusively academic).
1997: 8 titles.
ISBN Prefix(es): 1-879045; 1-58023
Send 6 1/2x9 1/2" envelope w/$1.01 postage for MS guidelines
Preferred form of initial contact: Proposal package containing outline, 3
    sample chapters, and cover letter explaining why project would fit
    our publishing program.
Send submissions to—
    Submissions Editor
Limitations/Restrictions: Include SASE if any part of submission should
    be returned to author.
Because of the individual consideration we give to each submission,
    response time may take up to 4 months. Follow-up calls are not
    useful before that point.

80   John Milton Society for the Blind

475 Riverside Dr, Room 455, New York, NY 10115
Fax: 212-870-3229
Managing Dir. & Ed.-in-Chief: Darcy Quigley
Assistant Editor: Ingrid Peck
Development & Circulation Manager: Sheila Mahoney
Faith/denominational/cultural focus: Christian
Subject areas: Prayer & Meditation, Missions, Spiritual Life/Personal
    Religion, Religion and the Family, Religious Biography, Theological
    Education (methodology), History of Religion(s), Religion in Popular
    Culture/Media, Biblical Literature — Commentary & Hermeneutics,
    Religious Education — Elementary, Religious Education —
    Secondary, Religious Education — Adult
Types of publications: Books-on-Tape, Reprints, Devotional Guides,
    Fiction — Adult, Fiction — Juvenile, Poetry, Braille, Large Print
The John Milton Society produces free magazines in Braille, large type,
    and on cassette for blind and visually impaired youth and adults.
    Most material is reprinted from various Christian periodicals with
    occasional previously unpublished pieces from individual authors.
    Our publications include: John Milton Magazine (large type), a
    digest of articles reprinted from a wide range of Christian
    periodicals; Adult Lessons Quarterly (Braille & cassette), a reprint of
    the Bible Discovery lessons based on the Uniform Series; and
    Discovery (Braille), a digest of reprinted articles for youth ages 8-18.
    Other materials include: Motto Calendar (Braille), annual Bible
    Study (Braille), worship services (large type), and a Directory of
    Resources (large type).
In print: 5 titles.
Send SASE for manuscript guidelines
Preferred form of initial contact: Proposal package containing SASE
    and complete manuscript.
Send submissions to—
    Darcy Quigley, Man. Dir. & Ed.-in-Chief
Limitations/Restrictions: Consult the magazines we typically reprint
    from. Submitted material must be complete with little or no editing
    required.
We cannot pay reprint fees to authors as all of our publications are free
    material for the blind.

81   The Johns Hopkins University Press

Subsidiary/division of The Johns Hopkins University
2715 N Charles Street, Baltimore, MD 21218-4319
Phone: 410-516-6900
Fax: 410-516-6968
WWW homepage: www.press.jhu.edu/real_home.html
Subject areas: Comparative Religions, History of Religion(s), Mythology, Sacred Languages, Religion and Classics, Religion and Cultural/Ethnic Studies, Religion and Gender Studies, Sociology of Religion, Anthropology of Religion, Religion and Archaeology, Religion and Economics, Religion and Political Science, Religion in Popular Culture/Media, Religion and Law, Sacred Literature — Cultural & Historical Contexts
Types of publications: Classroom Instructional Materials, General Interest Nonfiction — Adult, Translations, Scholarly Monographs, General Reference, Academic Reference
Acquisitions focus for 1998-9: Ancient Near Eastern religion, history of early Christianity, sociology of religion, and history of religion.
In print: 75 titles.   1997: 6 titles.
ISBN Prefix(es): 0-8108
Recent/Forthcoming Titles: Nadler, *The Faith of the Mithnagdim*; Guth, et al., *Uneasy in Zion: The New Religious Order in American Politics*; Haas, *Alexandria in Late Antiquity*
No manuscript guidelines available
Preferred form of initial contact: Proposal package containing outline and author's C.V.
Send submissions to—
   Henry Y. K. Tom, Executive Editor

82   Kar-Ben Copies, Inc

6800 Tildenwood Lane, Rockville, MD 20852
Phone: 800-452-7236
Fax: 301-881-9195
E-mail: karben@aol.com
WWW homepage: www.karben.com
President: Judye Groner
Vice President: Madeline Wikler
Faith/denominational/cultural focus: Judaism
Subject areas: Liturgy and Ritual, Religion and the Family, Folklore, Religious Education — Elementary

Types of publications: Classroom Instructional Materials, Illustrated Books, Fiction — Juvenile

Kar Ben publishes books on Jewish holidays, life cycle, folktales, cookbooks, activity books, and family services for High Holidays, Shabbat Sukkot. Popular titles include its children's Haggadah, *My Very Own Haggadah* and *A Family Haggadah*; the Sammy Spider series; a travel guide to Israel, *Kids Love Israel*; and the winner of the 1996 AJC Sydney Taylor award, *Shalom Haver, Goodbye Friend*, a tribute to Yitshak Rabin. Also publishes Jewish calendars.

In print: 95 titles.   1997: 6 titles.

ISBN Prefix(es): 0-930490, 0-92371, 1-58013

Recent/Forthcoming Titles: *Brainteasers from Jewish Folklore; All About Rosh Hashanah; All About Yom Kippur*

Manuscript guidelines free upon request.

Preferred form of initial contact: Proposal package containing SASE and full text of children's book (preschool - age 9; 3000 words max.)

Send submissions to—

Madeline Winkler, Vice President

Remember SASE and target to our niche.

83   Kazi Publications

3023 W Belmont Ave, Chicago, IL 60618

Phone: 773-267-7001

Fax: 773-267-7002

E-mail: kazibooks@kazi.org

WWW homepage: www.kazi.org

President: Liaquat Ali

Faith/denominational/cultural focus: Islam

Subject areas: Religious Life/Practice, Religious Thought/Theology, Religious Studies, Religion and Society, Koranic Literature, Religious Education

Types of publications: Classroom Instructional Materials, Liturgical Materials, General Interest Nonfiction — Adult, General Interest Nonfiction — Juvenile, 22, Self-Help, Scholarly Monographs, General Reference, Language Reference, Academic Reference

We publish books on all religious subject categories with special reference to Islam and Sufism.

In print: 300 titles.   1997: 6 titles.

10% of titles author-subsidized
ISBN Prefix(es): 1-871031, 0-935782, 0-933511, 1-56744
Recent/Forthcoming Titles:
Sufi Book of Spiritual Ascent; *Islam: Path of God*
Manuscript guidelines free upon request
Preferred form of initial contact: Proposal package containing complete
manuscript

84   Kimo Press

PO Box 82, Bellefonte, PA 16823
Phone: 814-355-8323
Fax: 814-355-4990
E-mail: kimopress@quaker.org
WWW homepage: www.kimopress.com
Publisher: Charles Foger
Faith/denominational/cultural focus: Society of Friends
Subject areas: Religious Life/Practice, Religious Thought/Theology,
  Mysticism, Religious Studies, Religion and Society, Sacred
  Literature, Religious Education
Types of publications: Classroom Instructional Materials, Books-on-
  Tape, Illustrated Books, Essay/Lecture Collections, Reprints,
  Devotional Guides, Fiction — Adult, Self-Help, Fiction — Juvenile
Materials about, relating, and of interest to members and attenders of
  The Religious Society of Friends, or Quakers. Our principal interests
  are in the liberal-unprogrammed Quaker tradition, but we are open
  to other varieties of Quakerism.
Acquisitions focus for 1998-9: Two new series: 1) The Best of Friends—
  superior writing, old and new, on Quaker topics; and 2) The Friendly
  Bible Commentary—volumes of approx. 100 pages on Biblical topics
  from a distinctly Quaker perspective.
In print: 12 titles.   1997: 2 titles.
Recent/Forthcoming Titles:
Words in Time; *The Best of Friends, Vol. 1* (anthology)

85   Kregel Publications

PO Box 2607, Grand Rapids, MI 49501

Phone: 616-451-4775

WWW homepage: kregel.com

Faith/denominational/cultural focus: Evangelical Christian

Subject areas: Prayer & Meditation, Preaching & Homiletics, Spiritual Life/Personal Religion, Religious Biography, Doctrinal Theology & Dogma, Systematic Theology, Theological Education (methodology), Religion in Popular Culture/Media, Religion and Law, Religion and Public Policy, Biblical Literature — Commentary & Hermeneutics, Biblical Literature — Translations, Religious Education — Theory and Methodology

Types of publications: Reprints, Devotional Guides, Fiction — Adult, Translations, General Reference, Academic Reference

Kregel Publications provides a variety of ministry tools for vocational Christian workers and clergy as well as Biblical studies and reference works for Bible colleges and seminaries. We also publish devotional works and works on contemporary issues for general readers.

Acquisitions focus for 1998-9: Contemporary issues, reference works, and pastoral helps.

In print: 550 titles.   1997: 60 titles.

ISBN Prefix(es): 0-8254

Recent/Forthcoming Titles: *Suicide: A Christian Response*; *Messiah's Coming Temple*; *Ethical Dilemmas in Church Leadership*

Manuscript guidelines free upon request

Preferred form of initial contact: Short query e-mailed to publisher.

Do not respond to complete manuscript proposals; do not usually read manuscripts sent without initial query.

86   KTAV Publishing House, Inc

900 Jefferson St, Hoboken, NJ 07030

Phone: 201-963-9524

Fax: 201-963-0102

E-mail: 74631.2017@compuserve.com

WWW homepage: www.ktav.com

President: Sol Scharfstein

Faith/denominational/cultural focus: Judaism

Subject areas: Religious Life/Practice, Religious Thought/Theology, Religious Studies, Religion and Society, Biblical Literature —

Translations, Talmudic Literature — Translations, Religious Education
Types of publications: Classroom Instructional Materials, Audio-Visual, Illustrated Books, Essay/Lecture Collections, Reprints, Devotional Guides, Liturgical Materials, General Interest Nonfiction — Adult, General Interest Nonfiction — Juvenile, Translations, Poetry, Scholarly Monographs, General Reference, Language Reference, Academic Reference
KTAV publishes and distributes prayer books, books for children and young adults, toys, games, school supplies, and textbooks. Additionally, KTAV publishes distinguished scholarly books which range from Biblical study to contemporary issues.
No manuscript guidelines available
Preferred form of initial contact:
Limitations/Restrictions: No fiction.

87   Legacy Press
Imprint of Rainbow Publishers
PO Box 261129, San Diego, CA 92196
Street Address: 9230 Trade Place, San Diego, CA 92126
Faith/denominational/cultural focus: Evangelical Christian
Subject areas: Prayer & Meditation, Spiritual Life/Personal Religion, Religion and the Family, Religious Education — Theory and Methodology, Religious Education — Elementary, Religious Education — Secondary, Religious Education — Adult
Types of publications: Illustrated Books, Devotional Guides, General Interest Nonfiction — Adult, General Interest Nonfiction — Juvenile
We publish Bible-based, Christ-centered materials that contribute to and inspire spiritual growth and development. This could include devotional books, Bible story books, or fresh takes on ways to live the Christian life most effectively. Our books are sold exclusively in the Christian bookstore market.
Acquisitions focus for 1998-9: Books for targeted demographic groups on Christian living (men, women, children, seniors, boomers, etc.)
In print: 8 titles. 1997: 3 titles.
Recent/Forthcoming Titles: *The Dickens Family Gospel*; *My Prayer Journal*; *Wisdom for Women*
Send SASE for manuscript guidelines

Preferred form of initial contact: Proposal package containing SASE, outline, 2-5 chapters, and author biography
Send submissions to—
Christy Allen, Editor
Research what is available in Christian bookstores before submitting a proposal; then tell us how your book fills a need in the market.

88   Light and Life Publishing Co
4818 Park Glen Rd, Minneapolis, MN 55416
Phone: 612-925-3888
Fax: 612-925-3918
Faith/denominational/cultural focus: Eastern Orthodox
Subject areas: Religious Life/Practice, Religious Thought/Theology, Religious Studies, Religion and Society, Sacred Literature (Eastern Orthodox), Religious Education
Types of publications: General Interest Nonfiction — Adult, General Reference
Light and Life publishes on spirituality, Church Fathers, early Church, the Orthodox Church: its history, faith, and life.
In print: 150 titles.   1997: 12 titles.
10% of titles author-subsidized
ISBN Prefix(es): 1-880-971
Recent/Forthcoming Titles: *Becoming Uncreated: The Journey to Human Authenticity; Dictionary of Greek Orthodoxy; Finding God in Times of Sorrow and Despair*
No manuscript guidelines available
No unsolicited submissions accepted

89   Liguori Publications
One Liguori Drive, Liguori, MO 63057
Triumph Liguori: 333 Glenhead Rd, Suite 260, Old Brookville, NY 11545
Phone: 314-464-2500, 516-759-7402 (Triumph Liguori)
Fax: 314-464-8449, 516-759-8619 (Triumph Liguori)
WWW homepage: www.liguori.org
Faith/denominational/cultural focus: Roman Catholic
Subject areas: Prayer & Meditation, Spiritual Life/Personal Religion, Religion & Family, Religion & Health, Religious Biography, Ethics

Types of publications: Essay/Lecture Collections, Devotional Guides, General Interest Nonfiction — Adult, Self-Help

Liguori publishes hard cover and paperback originals and reprints under the Ligouri and Triumph imprints in the following areas: nonfiction, inspirational, devotional, prayer, Christian-living, self-help, and contemporary religious issues, all with Catholic Christian emphasis.

Acquisitions focus for 1998-9: Prayer, Christian-living, devotional: manuscripts of 150-200 pages.

In print: 135 titles.   1997: 28 titles.

ISBN Prefix(es): 0-7648

Recent/Forthcoming Titles: *How Can I Find God?*; *Mother Teresa: In My Own Words*; *The Essential Catholic Handbook*

Manuscript guidelines free upon request

Preferred form of initial contact: Proposal package containing SASE, outline, 2-4 sample chapters.

Send submissions to—

New York office (Triumph): Patricia Kossmann, Executive Editor
Anthony Chiffolo, Managing Editor
Judith Bauer, Editor

Looking for unpublished authors who write beautifully with something new to say. Consult our list and tailor your writing to our audience.

90   The Liturgical Press

PO Box 7500, St John's Abbey, Collegeville, MN 56321
Phone: 320-363-2213
Fax: 320-363-3299
WWW homepage: www.litpress.org
Publisher: Michael Naughton
Managing Editor: Mark Twomey
Marketing Manager: Peter Dwyer
Financial Manager: Jerry Furst
Faith/denominational/cultural focus: Roman Catholic
Subject areas: Liturgy and Ritual, Preaching & Homiletics, Doctrinal Theology & Dogma, Systematic Theology, Pastoral Theology, Theological Education (Methodology), Pluralistic/Ecumenical Theology, Benedictine Studies, Monastic Studies

Types of publications: Essay/Lecture Collections, Devotional Guides, Liturgical Materials, General Interest Nonfiction — Adult, Academic Reference

Editorial vision: scripture, liturgy, theology, and monastic spirituality provide the well-spring for the publication of quality materials for both pastoral and academic audiences.

In print: 900 titles.   1997: 85 titles.

5% of titles author-subsidized

ISBN Prefix(es): 0-8146

Recent/Forthcoming Titles: *The Collegeville Bible Handbook; The Encyclopedia of American Catholic History; Handbook for Liturgical Studies, vol. 1*

Manuscript guidelines free upon request

Preferred form of initial contact: Proposal package containing SASE, outline, 1 sample chapter, and cover letter stating focus of manuscript and defining its readership

91   Liturgy Training Publications

1800 N Hermitage Ave, Chicago, IL 60622-1101

Phone: 773-486-8970

Fax: 773-486-7094

E-mail: editors@ltp.org

Director: Gabe Huck

General Manager: John Wright

Senior Acquisitions Editor: Victoria Tufano

Faith/denominational/cultural focus: Roman Catholic, liturgical Christianity

Subject areas: Liturgy and Ritual, Prayer & Meditation, Preaching & Homiletics, Spiritual Life/Personal Religion, Religion and the Family, Religious Biography, Religious Architecture

Types of publications: Classroom Instructional Materials, Illustrated Books, Essay/Lecture Collections, Reprints, Devotional Guides, Liturgical Materials, Scholarly Monographs

We publish materials aimed primarily at assisting those who have responsibility for implementing the liturgy and prayer life of the Church in Roman Catholic (and other Christian) churches (e.g., pastors, liturgists, musicians, decorators, sacristans, and committee members) and homes (e.g., parents). Materials are based on Vatican II principles and subsequent documents. Some materials are also directed at a more scholarly level and some are directed toward the average parishioner or volunteer.

Acquisitions focus for 1998-9: We will be focusing on books for each of the liturgical ministries; books for those who work in Hispanic parishes, both in English and Spanish; some 'spirituality' of liturgy.

In print: 300 titles.   1997: 30 titles.

ISBN Prefix(es): 0-929650, 0-930467, 1-56854

Recent/Forthcoming Titles: *Eucharistic Prayer at Sunday Mass*; *A Reconciliation Sourcebook*; *Child of God: A Book for Birthdays and Days in Between*

Manuscript guidelines free upon request

Preferred form of initial contact: Proposal package containing short query, SASE, outline, sample chapters, and description of audience and purpose.

Send submissions to—

Church building, renovating, and decorating: David Philippart, Acquisitions Editor

Christian initiation, general liturgy, everything else: Victoria Tufano, Senior Acquisitions Editor

Limitations/Restrictions: No books of sermons/homilies or devotionals. Materials must fall within the confines of current Roman Catholic discipline.

Most of our authors are teachers or practitioners in the area of liturgy, as our editors.

92   Longwood Communications

397 Kingslake Drive, DeBary, FL 32713

Phone: 904-774-2144

Fax: 904-724-8181

E-mail: longwood@totcon.com

Faith/denominational/cultural focus: Evangelical Christian

Subject areas: Prayer & Meditation, Missions, Spiritual Life/Personal Religion, Religion and the Family, Religion and Health, Religious Biography, Religion and Law

Types of publications: Reprints, Devotional Guides, General Interest Nonfiction — Adult, Fiction — Adult, Self-Help

Longwood Communications publishes books for the Evangelical Christian market; we are looking for books that build-up as opposed to argumentative works.

In print: 32 titles.   1997: 8 titles.
100% of titles author-subsidized
ISBN Prefix(es): 883928
Recent/Forthcoming Titles: *Holy to Yahweh*; *Mrs. Miracle*; *Reclaiming Our Youth*
Brochure free upon request
Preferred form of initial contact: Proposal package containing SASE, single-sided, double spaced manuscript
Send submissions to—
    Murray Fisher, Vice President

93   Mayfield Publishing
1280 Villa St, Mountain View, CA 94041
Phone: 415-433-1279
Fax: 415-960-0826
WWW homepage: mayfield.com
Subject areas: Ethics, Comparative Religions, Philosophy of Religion, Religious Education — Theory and Methodology
Types of publications: Classroom Instructional Materials
Aim to publish for the post-secondary market in religious studies curriculum, whether taught in philosophy or separate religious studies programs. We publish undergraduate texts exclusively. Must be aimed at presently existing courses.
Recent/Forthcoming Titles: Molloy, *World Religions*; Saint-Laurent, *Spirituality*; Kessler, *World Religions*
Manuscript guidelines free upon request
Preferred form of initial contact: Short written query with a proposal
Limitations/Restrictions: Outline of proposed texts should conform to the organization most teachers follow in presenting their courses.

94   Mercer University Press
Subsidiary/division of Mercer University
6316 Peake Road, Macon, GA 31210-3960
Mercer University: 1400 Coleman Ave, Macon, GA 31207
Phone: 912-752-2880
Fax: 912-752-2264

E-mail: mupressorders@mercer.edu
WWW homepage: mercer.edu/~mupress
Publisher: Dr. Cecil P. Staton, Jr.
Assistant Publisher: Dr. Marc A. Jolley
Faith/denominational/cultural focus: Christian
Subject areas: Religious Biography, Religious Thought/Theology, Comparative Religions, History of Religion(s), Sacred Languages, Interdisciplinary Studies, Religion in Popular Culture/Media, Religion and Law, Sacred Literature — Commentary & Hermeneutics, Sacred Literature — Cultural & Historical Contexts, Sacred Literature — Translations
Types of publications: Essay/Lecture Collections, Reprints, Scholarly Monographs, General Reference, Academic Reference
We consider for publication serious works of scholarship in the general field of religious/theological studies. We do not publish sermons, devotional guides, etc. Works of history are especially considered, as are works in biblical and theological studies. Philosophy of religion (Kierkegaard, Kant, & Tillich) is also a strong area of our program.
Acquisitions focus for 1998-9: Biblical, philosophical, theological, and historical monographs; history of religion, especially religion of the American South.
In print: 200 titles.   1997: 20 titles.
ISBN Prefix(es): 0-86554
Recent/Forthcoming Titles: Thomas Helwys, *A Short Declaration of the Mystery of Iniquity*; Herrmann Gunkel, *Genesis* (trans.); Fritz Buri, *The Buddha-Christ*
Manuscript guidelines free upon request
Preferred form of initial contact: Short written query or proposal package containing outline, at least 2 chapters, and author's C.V.
Send submissions to—
    Gen'l Biblical, theological: Marc A. Jolley, Assistant Publisher
    Gen'l religion, Biblical, philosophy of religion: Edmon L. Rowell, Jr., Senior Editor
    History of religion, church history, history of southern religion: Andrew Manis, Editor

95   Ministry Publications
Subsidiary/division of Ministry of the Word, Inc
7135 E Sunnyside Drive, Scottsdale, AZ 85254
Mailing: PO Box 12222, Scottsdale, AZ 85267
Phone: 602-948-4050, 800-573-4105 (orders)
Fax: 602-922-1338
E-mail: MinWord12@aol.com
WWW homepage: thechristian.org
President: William T. Freeman
Secretary/Treasurer: Robert K. Eland
Faith/denominational/cultural focus: Christian
Subject areas: Prayer & Meditation, Spiritual Life/Personal Religion,
    Doctrinal Theology & Dogma
Types of publications: Electronic Publications (Internet), Devotional
    Guides, Spiritual Growth
Ministry Publications publishes books and booklets, including a daily
    devotional; books on the Christian life and spiritual growth; studies
    of the Bible; and various aids and workbooks to support study of the
    Bible as it applies to the Christian life.
In print: 30 titles.   1997: 6 titles.
ISBN Prefix(es): 9-14271
Recent/Forthcoming Titles: *The Kingdom Life; God as All in All; Focus
    in the Christian Life*
No manuscript guidelines available
No unsolicited submissions accepted

96   Moody Press
Subsidiary/division of Moody Bible Institute
820 N LaSalle Blvd, Chicago, IL 60610
Phone: 312-329-2101, 800-678-8812 (orders)
Fax: 312-329-8062, 800-678-3329 (orders)
E-mail: pressinfo@moody.edu
WWW homepage: www.moodypress.org
VP, Publications: Greg Thornton
Faith/denominational/cultural focus: Evangelical Christian
Subject areas: Prayer & Meditation, Spiritual Life/Personal Religion,
    Religion and the Family
Types of publications: Illustrated Books, Devotional Guides, General
    Interest Nonfiction — Adult, General Interest Nonfiction — Juvenile

We produce books that educate, edify, and evangelize. We rarely do reprints. We're not currently seeking scholarly books, dissertations, poetry, fiction, personal experience stories, Bible studies, short stories, sermons, or cookbooks. We primarily publish general Christian living books for the broad market of CBA readers. Our books address finance, family, Christian living, and children

Acquisitions focus for 1998-9: Developing current authors while remaining open to 1-2 new authors.

In print: 700 titles.   1997: 70 titles.

1% of titles author-subsidized

ISBN Prefix(es): 0-8024

Recent/Forthcoming Titles: *The ABC's of Wisdom*; *The Five Love Languages of Children*; *Lasting Love*

Send #10 SASE for manuscript guidelines

Preferred form of initial contact: Proposal package containing SASE, outline, 2-3 sample chapters, author biography, and market study.

Send submissions to—

Acquisitions Coordinator

Limitations/Restrictions: Less than 1% of unsolicited material is published by Moody Press each year.

Use the Evangelical Christian Pubs Association's First Edition internet service for submission to all member presses (www.ecpa.org). Send 9x12" SASE (3 oz. postage) to receive our catalog.

97   Morehouse Publishing

Subsidiary/division of Morehouse Group

Box 1321, Harrisburg, PA 17110

Street: 4775 Linglestown Rd, Harrisburg, PA 17110

Phone: 717-541-8130

Fax: 717-541-8136

Publisher: Harold Rast

President: Ken Quigley

VP Sales & Marketing: Leslie Merrell

Faith/denominational/cultural focus: Episcopal, Christian

Subject areas: Religious Life/Practice, Pastoral Theology, Pluralistic & Ecumenical Theology, Religion in Popular Culture/Media, Religion and Public Policy, Religious Education — Theory and Methodology, Religious Education — Public policy/Legal Issues

Types of publications: Classroom Instructional Materials, Devotional Guides, Liturgical Materials, General Interest Nonfiction — Adult, Self-Help, Fiction — Juvenile, Poetry

Morehouse publishes books of interest in the Episcopal market, as well as books of general interest to the mainline Christian market as a whole. Areas of greatest interest include spirituality and the interaction of spirituality with life, health, etc., as well as books of practical value to Christians, and books of interest to the institutional church. Unusual children's books are sought that emphasize Christian themes.

1997: 40 titles.

ISBN Prefix(es): 0-8192

Recent/Forthcoming Titles: *Assisted Suicide & Euthanasia*; *God Works*; *A Pastor's Survival Guide*

Manuscript guidelines free upon request

Preferred form of initial contact: Proposal package containing SASE, outline, sample chapters, author biography, and analysis of book's market position.

Send submissions to—

Debra K. Farrington, Editorial Director

98   Mount Olive College Press

Subsidiary/division of Mount Olive College

634 Henderson St, Mount Olive, NC 28365

Phone: 919-658-2502

Faith/denominational/cultural focus: Free-Will Baptist

Subject areas: Prayer & Meditation, Preaching & Homiletics, Spiritual Life/Personal Religion, Ethics, Religious Education — Theory and Methodology

Types of publications: Music, Essay/Lecture Collections, General Interest Nonfiction — Adult, Fiction — Adult, Poetry

The Mount Olive College Press seeks to publish inspirational stories, essays, novels, poetry, and music: material that has a quality of theological thoughtfulness and applied wisdom.

In print: 41 titles.

Recent/Forthcoming Titles: Bonnie Blue Barton, *Mother I Have AIDS*; Wilbur L. Creech, *The Scalpel and the Cross*; Dr. De Wayne Eakes, *The Crisis of Leadership*

Send SASE for manuscript guidelines

Preferred form of initial contact: Proposal package containing SASE and 2 sample chapters.

Send submissions to—

Dr. Pepper Worthington, Editor-in-Chief

Limitations/Restrictions: Manuscript submissions will not be returned. We do reply within 2 to 4 months.

99   New City Press

Subsidiary/division of Focolare Movement

202 Cardinal Road, Hyde Park, NY 12538

Phone: 914-229-0335

Fax: 914-229-0351

E-mail: ncporder@aol.com

Business Manager: Bob Cummings

Production Manager: Nick Cianfarani

Editor: Jerry Hearne

Faith/denominational/cultural focus: Christian

Subject areas: Prayer & Meditation, Preaching & Homiletics, Spiritual Life/Personal Religion, Religious Biography, Focolare Spirituality, Comparative Religions, Religious Education — Post-Secondary, Religious Education — Seminary, Religious Education — Adult

Types of publications: Classroom Instructional Materials, Liturgical Materials, General Interest Nonfiction — Adult, Translations, Self-Help, Academic Reference

New City Press promotes spiritual works of all Christian eras, including a series on the spirituality of the Fathers, selected spiritual writings of the spiritual masters of the middle ages, and publications of contemporary spirituality (with an emphasis on the Focolare movement's spirituality of unity). Its scholarly programs already feature the works of Saint Augustine and Saint Vincent de Paul, while in preparation are the early biographical documents of Saint Francis.

Acquisitions focus for 1998-9: Theology and interreligious dialogue from the perspective of an ecclesial communitarian spirituality.

In print: 102 titles.   1997: 9 titles.

20% of titles author-subsidized

ISBN Prefix(es): 1-56548

Recent/Forthcoming Titles: Chiara Zubrich, *Christian Living Today: Meditations*; Daniel Harrington, *Romans: The Good News*

According to Paul; Judith Zang, *The Angels of God: Understanding Angels through Scripture*
Preferred form of initial contact: Proposal package containing SASE, outline, 1 sample chapter.
Acquisitions address: 86 Mayflower Ave, New Rochelle, NY 10801
Do not send complete manuscripts (on paper or diskettes) or audio tapes.

100   New York University Press

70 Washington Square South, New York, NY 10012
Phone: 212-998-2575, 800-996-6987 (customer service/orders)
Fax: 212-995-3833
WWW homepage: www.nyupress.nyu.edu
Subject areas: History of Religion(s), Religion and Cultural/Ethnic Studies, Religion and Gender Studies, Psychology of Religion, Sociology of Religion, Anthropology of Religion, Religion and Economics, Religion and Political Science, Religion in Popular Culture/Media, Religion and Law, Religion and Public Policy, Sacred Literature — Cultural & Historical Contexts
Types of publications: Essay/Lecture Collections, General Interest Nonfiction — Adult, Scholarly Monographs
New York University Press publishes projects relating to religion and American culture and history, gender and religion; religion, race, and ethnicity; and Jewish studies. While most of our list focuses on the U.S., we also publish several titles on religion in other parts of the world (i.e. books looking at the Islamist challenge in Algeria, fundamentalism in Afghanistan, etc.).
Acquisitions focus for 1998-9: While we will continue to publish in each of the areas named above, we will be particularly interested in looking at projects examining religion in American culture, history, law and education; gender and religion; religion, race, and ethnicity; and Jewish studies.
In print: 108 titles.   1997: 13 titles.   ISBN Prefix(es): 0-8147
Recent/Forthcoming Titles: Daniel Wojcik, *The End of the World as We Know it: Faith, Fatalism and Apocalypse in America*; Oran P. Smith, *The Rise of Baptist Republicanism*; Ezra Mendelsohn, ed., *Essential Papers on Jews and the Left*
Manuscript guidelines free upon request
Preferred form of initial contact: Proposal package containing outline, 3-4 sample chapters, and C.V.
Send submissions to—Jennifer Hammer, Associate Editor

101   Nilgiri Press
Subsidiary/division of Blue Mountain Center of Meditation
PO Box 256, 3600 Tomales Rd, Tomales, CA 94971
Phone: 707-878-2369
Fax: 707-878-2375
E-mail: info@BMCM.org
WWW homepage: www.nilgiri.org
Subject areas: Prayer & Meditation, Spiritual Life/Personal Religion,
    Religion and the Family, Religion and Health, Religious Biography,
    Comparative Religions, Religion and Classics, Sacred Literature —
    Commentary & Hermeneutics, Tantric/Vedic Lit. — Commentary &
    Hermeneutics, Buddhist Literature — Translations
Types of publications: Illustrated Books, Essay/Lecture Collections,
    General Interest Nonfiction — Adult, Translations, inspirational
Nilgiri Press publishes books, audio, and video tapes on meditation and
    spiritual growth that give practical guidance for bringing high ideals
    to life. They include commentaries on the works of mystics,
    biographies of outstanding spiritual figures, translations and
    commentaries on the scriptures of the major religions, daily
    inspirational readers, wise tales for children, and books exploring
    death. Drawing from both eastern and western traditions, they
    provide a universal perspective useful for any who desire to deepen
    their spirituality within their own cultural and religious
    backgrounds.
In print: 24 titles.   1997: 2 titles.
ISBN Prefix(es): 0-915132, 1-888314
Recent/Forthcoming Titles: *Seeing with the Eyes of Love*; *Love Never
    Faileth*; *Original Goodness*
No manuscript guidelines available
Preferred form of initial contact: No unsolicited submissions accepted.

102   Orbis Books
Subsidiary/division of Catholic Foreign Mission Society of America
Maryknoll, NY 10545
Phone: 914-941-7590
Fax: 914-945-0670
E-mail: Orbisbooks@aol.com
Executive Director: Robert Gormley
Editor-in-Chief: Robert Ellsberg

Faith/denominational/cultural focus: Roman Catholic
Subject areas: Prayer & Meditation, Preaching & Homiletics, Missions, Spiritual Life/Personal Religion, Religious Biography, Ethics, Doctrinal Theology & Dogma, Systematic Theology, Pastoral Theology, Theological Education (methodology), Pluralistic/Ecumenical Theology, Comparative Religions, History of Religion(s), Religion and Art, Religion and Music, Religion and Literature, Religion and Cultural/Ethnic Studies, Religion and Gender Studies, Religion and Economics, Religion and Public Policy, Biblical Literature — Commentary & Hermeneutics, Biblical Literature — Cultural & Historical Contexts, Religious Education — Theory and Methodology
Types of publications: Classroom Instructional Materials, Illustrated Books, Essay/Lecture Collections, Reprints, General Interest Nonfiction — Adult, Translations, Scholarly Monographs, Dissertations, General Reference, Academic Reference
Global dimensions of Christian faith, including issues of religious pluralism, the relation between faith and culture, mission, and the struggle for peace and justice. Specialties include theology, Biblical studies, ethics, interreligious dialogue, spirituality, and mission; classroom texts as well as for individual scholars. Includes both academic books and works for the general reader.
Acquisitions focus for 1998-9: Textbooks in ethics and theology, including feminist, African-American studies, ecology, and mission theology. Also reference works.
In print: 400 titles.   1997: 50 titles.
5% of titles author-subsidized
ISBN Prefix(es): 0-88344; 1-57075
Recent/Forthcoming Titles: Giusseppe Alberigo, *History of Vatican II*; Ursula King, *Spirit of Fire: The Life of Teilhard de Chardin*; Larry Rasmussen, *Earth Community, Earth Ethics*
Manuscript guidelines free upon request
Preferred form of initial contact: Short written query
Send submissions to—
    Mission, interreligious dialogue, ecology, academic theology: Bill Burrows, Managing Editor
    Ethics, feminist theology, African theology:
        Susan Perry, Senior Editor
    Black theology, Biblical studies, liberation theology, spirituality:
        Robert Ellsberg, Ed

103   Oughten House Publications
PO Box 2008, Livermore, CA 94551-2008
Phone: 888-673-3748 (orders)
E-mail: oughtenhouse.com
WWW homepage: www.oughtenhouse.com
Publisher & CEO: Robert V. Gerard
Dir. of Marketing: Anita Jarrett Gerard
Dir. of Operations & Ed.-in-Chief: Tony Stubbs
Subject areas: Prayer & Meditation, Spiritual Life/Personal Religion, Religion and Health, Philosophy of Religion, Psychology of Religion, Sociology of Religion, Religion and the Physical Sciences, Religion and the Natural Sciences
Types of publications: Fiction — Adult, Poetry, General Reference
Oughten House focuses on spiritual works with respect to all religions and mature cultures. All our books reinforce the positive orientations to mankind, then planet and God. We do not tolerate fear-based information, rather advocate literature that professes hope and inspiration. Several books by highly credentialed and public scientists in science and metaphysics, as well as health are in production.
Acquisitions focus for 1998-9: Nine books already planned for 1997. For 1998-99, we seek very basic entry-level books on spirituality and personal growth, including books on bridging the gap between science, health, and metaphysics.
1997: 1 title.
10% of titles author-subsidized
ISBN Prefix(es): 1-880666
Recent/Forthcoming Titles: *Revelations Revised*
Send #10 SASE for manuscript guidelines
Preferred form of initial contact: Proposal package containing synopsis outline; the first two and final chapters; marketing plan, author biography and credentials, as well as SASE.
Send submissions to—
   Ms. Joy Marie, Title Acquisitions
Limitations/Restrictions: All work must be well (professionally) presented; send no original artwork—copies only.
Please review our web site (www.oughtenhouse.com) before submitting materials; verify that we are the publisher which can best serve your needs and best promote your book in the genre of mutual interest.

104   Oxford University Press
198 Madison Ave, New York, NY 10016
Order Dept.: Oxford University Press, 2001 Evans Rd, Cary, NC 27513
Phone: 212-726-6000, 800-451-7556 (orders), 800-455-9714 (Cust. Svc.)
Fax: 919-677-1303 (orders)
WWW homepage: www.oup-usa.org
Editorial Assistant: Gene Romanosky
Subject areas: Liturgy and Ritual, Prayer & Meditation, Religion and
    Health, Religious Biography, Ethics, Doctrinal Theology & Dogma,
    Systematic Theology, Pastoral Theology, Natural Theology,
    Theological Education (Methodology), Pluralistic/Ecumenical
    Theology, Comparative Religions, History of Religion(s),
    Mythology, Folklore, Sacred Languages, Interdisciplinary Studies,
    Methodologies of Study and Teaching, Religion and Society, Sacred
    Literature
Types of publications: Electronic Publications, Music, Essay/Lecture
    Collections, Reprints, General Interest Nonfiction — Adult,
    Translations, Scholarly Monographs, General Reference, Language
    Reference, Academic Reference
We publish in all areas of religious studies. However, we do not publish
    devotional books. We publish academic and trade books, college
    texts, academic and trade reference books, and music. We have a
    Children's Department that primarily publishes nonfiction and
    reference books for children and young adults.
In print: 840 titles.   1997: 80 titles.
ISBN Prefix(es): 0-19-5 (U.S.); 0-19-8 (UK)
Recent/Forthcoming Titles: Michael W. Cuneo, *The Smoke of Satan:*
    Conservative and Traditionalist Dissent in Contemporary American
    Catholicism; Byron L. Sherwin, *Sparks Amidst the Ashes: The*
    Spiritual Legacy of Polish Jewry; Yvonne Yazbeck Haddad & John L.
    Esposito (eds.), *Islam, Gender, and Social Change*
No manuscript guidelines available.
Preferred form of initial contact: Proposal package containing SASE,
    outline, 2 sample chapters, and author's C.V.
Send submissions to—
    Academic & trade books: Cynthia Read, Executive Editor
    College texts: Robert Miller, Executive Editor
    Trade reference: Linda Morse, Editorial Director
    Scholarly reference: Christopher Collins, Senior Editor
    Electronic publishing: Laura Calderone, New Media Editor
    Music: Maribeth Payne, Executive Editor

105   P & R Publishing
PO Box 817, Phillipsburg, NJ 08865-0817
Phone: 908-454-0505
Fax: 908-859-2390
President: Bryce H. Craig
Editor: Thom E. Notaro
Faith/denominational/cultural focus: Protestant, Reformed
Subject areas: Preaching & Homiletics, Missions, Spiritual Life/Personal Religion, Religion and the Family, Ethics, Doctrinal Theology & Dogma, Systematic Theology, Biblical Literature — Commentary & Hermeneutics, Biblical Literature — Cultural & Historical Contexts
Types of publications: Essay/Lecture Collections, Reprints, General Interest Nonfiction — Adult
P & R Publishing Company is dedicated to publishing excellent books that promote Biblical understanding and godly living as summarized in The Westminster Confession of Faith and Catechisms. Our mission is to serve Christ and his church by producing clear, engaging, fresh, and insightful applications of Reformed theology to life. We focus on non-fiction for the following audiences: the Christian bookstore/popular market, adult Sunday school/educated laypeople, and the pastoral/seminary level. Our titles range from academic works advancing Biblical and theological scholarship to popular books designed to help lay readers grow in Christian thought and service.
In print: 185 titles.   1997: 11 title.
ISBN Prefix(es): 0-87552
Recent/Forthcoming Titles: John M. Frame, *Contemporary Worship Music: A Biblical Defense*; Edward T. Welch, *When People Are Big and God Is Small: Overcoming Peer Pressure, Codependency, and the Fear of Man*; Ernest C. Reisinger, *The Law and the Gospel*
Manuscript guidelines free upon request
Preferred form of initial contact: Proposal package containing short query, SASE, outline, and description of chapters.
Send submissions to—
    Barbara Lerch, Acquisitions
Limitations/Restrictions: No personal accounts, humor, or juvenile materials. Please review our catalog before submitting a proposal.

106   Paraclete Press
Subsidiary/division of Creative Joys, Inc
PO Box 1568, Orleans, MA 02653
Phone: 508-255-4685
Fax: 508-255-5705
E-mail: mail@paraclete-press.com
WWW homepage: www.paraclete-press.com
Director of Marketing: Carol D. Showalter
Executive Secretary: Sr. Mercy Minor
Faith/denominational/cultural focus: Christian
Subject areas: Prayer & Meditation, Spiritual Life/Personal Religion,
    Sacred Literature — New Editions
Types of pubns: Reprints, Devotional Guides, Christian Spirituality
Paraclete Press publishes new editions of Christian classics,
    devotionals, books on spirituality, contributions to interfaith
    dialogue, and modern classics of depth.
In print: 45 titles.   1997: 9 titles.
ISBN Prefix(es): 1-55725
Recent/Forthcoming Titles: *How Firm a Foundation: A Gift of Jewish
    Wisdom for Christians and Jews; So Amazing, So Divine: A Guide to
    Living Prayer*
Send SASE w/3 oz. 1st class postage for manuscript guidelines
Preferred form of initial contact: Proposal package containing SASE
    and outline.
Send submissions to—
    Sr. Mercy Minor, Executive Secretary
Limitations/Restrictions: We do not publish poetry, children's books, or
    New Age philosophy.

107   Paragon House Publishers
2700 University Ave W, Suite 200, St. Paul, MN 55114
Phone: 612-644-3087
Fax: 612-644-0997
E-mail: gordon@pwpa.org
WWW homepage: www.pwpa.org/Paragon
Rights & Permissions: Laureen Enright
Faith/denominational/cultural focus: Judaism, Interfaith
Subject areas: Spiritual Life/Personal Religion, Religion and the
    Family, Ethics, Pluralistic/Ecumenical Theology, Comparative

Religions, Interdisciplinary Studies, Religion and Society, Sacred
Literature — Translations

Types of publications: Classroom Instructional Materials, Self-Help,
Scholarly Monographs, General Reference, Academic Reference

Paragon House publishes broadly in religion with an emphasis on
scholarly works that bring an understanding of the value of religious
practices in modern life and universal principles towards which
religion strives. Paragon House publishes works on the great
religious traditions, comparative religion, religious dialogue and
spiritual development.

Acquisitions focus for 1998-9: Religion and society, creation, universal
principles.

In print: 100 titles.   1997: 10 titles.

ISBN Prefix(es): 1-55778, 0-913757, 0-943852

Recent/Forthcoming Titles: *Proverbs of Africa*; *Evil and the Response of
World Religions*; *The Family in Global Transition*

Manuscript guidelines free upon request

Preferred form of initial contact: Proposal package containing SASE,
outline, 1 sample chapter, estimated no. of pages and date of
completion.

Send submissions to—
 General religion, world religion: Thomas G. Walsh
 Religion and society: Gordon L. Anderson

108   The Pastoral Press
Subsidiary/division of Trinity Music, Inc
PO Box 1470, Laurel, MD 20725
Phone: 301-725-0990, 800-976-9669 (orders)
Fax: 301-725-0941, 800-979-9669 (orders)
E-mail: publisher@pastoralpress.com
WWW homepage: pastoralpress.com
Editor: Larry Johnson
Publisher: Mindie Santi
Faith/denominational/cultural focus: Roman Catholic
Subject areas: Liturgy and Ritual, Prayer & Meditation, Process
Theology, Pastoral Theology, Theological Education (Methodology),
Religion and Art, Religion and Music, Religious Education — Adult

Types of publications: Classroom Instructional Materials, Audio-Visual, Music, Liturgical Materials, General Interest Nonfiction — Adult, Scholarly Monographs, General Reference

The Pastoral Press publishes books, music, video and audio cassettes that support training programs and resources for pastoral ministry in the Catholic Church. All lay and clerical ministries are supported. The Pastoral Press also publishes books on theological and scholarly studies particularly those addressing liturgy and ritual. We carry several texts addressing women's studies and texts on spiritual development and enrichment.

Acquisitions focus for 1998-9: Spiritual development (personal and evangelical), youth ministry.

In print: 168 titles.   1997: 6 titles.

ISBN Prefix(es): 1-56929, 0-97405

Recent/Forthcoming Titles: *The Seven Lost Words of Christ; Classroom Prayer Basics; A View from the Bridge*

Manuscript guidelines free upon request

Preferred form of initial contact: Proposal package containing SASE, outline, sample chapter.

Send submissions to—
Larry Johnson, Editor

109   Pauline Books & Media
50 St. Paul's Ave, Boston, MA 02130
Phone: 617-522-8911, 800-876-4463 (orders)
Fax: 617-541-9805, 617-524-8035 (orders)
E-mail: pbm_edit@interramp.com
WWW homepage: www.pauline.org
Faith/denominational/cultural focus: Roman Catholic
Subject areas: Liturgy and Ritual, Prayer & Meditation, Spiritual Life/Personal Religion, Religion and the Family, Religious Biography lives of the Saints, Biblical Literature — Commentary & Hermeneutics Biblical spirituality & pastoral Biblical studies, Religious Education — Elementary, Religious Education — Adult, Religion Teachers' Resources, Writings of the Pope, Documents of the Catholic

Types of publications: Classroom Instructional Materials, Books-on-Tape, Audio-Visual, Electronic Publications CD-ROM, Music, Illustrated Books, Devotional Guides, Liturgical Materials, Self-Help, Fiction — Juvenile, Prayer Books, Pamphlets

Pauline Books & Media is a Roman Catholic publishing house which seeks to communicate and promote Gospel values through all available forms of media. We give preference to manuscript submissions which are intended for the ordinary reader/viewer/listener, are pastoral in nature, faithful to the teachings of the Catholic church, and promote the integral advancement of the human person.

Acquisitions focus for 1998-9: Mariology; lives of Saints; popular presentations of the Catholic faith for adults (small pamphlets & paperbacks); specifically Catholic children's books (lives of saints, Marian, prayers, Eucharist-related); children's Lenten, Easter and Christmas books; books/pamphlets on grieving from a faith perspective; books on coping/healing.

In print: 800 titles.   1997: 20 titles.

ISBN Prefix(es): 0-8198

Recent/Forthcoming Titles: *Favorite Prayers and Novenas*; *My First Book about Mary (children's)*; *The Christmas Creche: Treasure of Faith, Art and Theater*

Send SASE for manuscript guidelines

Preferred form of initial contact: Proposal package containing SASE, outline, and 3 sample chapters.

Send submissions to—

    All books: Sr. Mary Mark, F.S.P, Acquisitions/Books
    Cassettes, music & spoken word: Sr. Bridget Charles, F.S.P., Acquisitions/Audio
    Videos: Sr. Marie Paul, F.S.P., Acquisitions/Video
    Software: Sr. Rose Pacatte, F.S.P., Acquisitions/Software

Limitations/Restrictions: No poetry, adult fiction, autobiographical works, or anthropomorphic children's books. All manuscripts must be consonant with Catholic theology.

Please make all queries in writing, not via phone.

110   Paulist Press

997 Macarthur Blvd, Mahwah, NJ 07430
Phone: 201-825-7300, 800-218-1903 (orders)
Fax: 201-825-8345, 800-836-3161 (orders)
E-mail: paulistp@usa.pipeline.com
WWW homepage: paulistpress.com
Publisher: Kevin A. Lynch, CSP
Marketing Director: John A. Thomas
Faith/denominational/cultural focus: Roman Catholic, Ecumenical
Subject areas: Religious Life/Practice, Religious Thought/Theology, Comparative Religions, History of Religion(s), Mythology, Religion and Literature, Religion and Cultural/Ethnic Studies, Religion and Gender Studies, Psychology of Religion, Sociology of Religion, Anthropology of Religion, Religion and Archaeology, Religion and Political Science, Religion and the Physical Sciences, Religion and the Natural Sciences, Religion in Popular Culture/Media, Religion and Public Policy, Biblical Literature — Commentary & Hermeneutics, Biblical Literature — Cultural & Historical Contexts, Talmudic Literature — Commentary & Hermeneutics, Talmudic Literature — Cultural & Historical Contexts, Koranic Literature — Commentary & Hermeneutics, Koranic Literature — Cultural & Historical Contexts, Religious Education — Theory and Methodology, Religious Education — Secondary, Religious Education — Post-Secondary, Religious Ed. — Seminary, Religious Education — Adult
Types of publications: Classroom Instructional Materials, Audio-Visual, Essay/Lecture Collections, Devotional Guides, Liturgical Materials, General Interest Nonfiction — Adult, Self-Help, Fiction — Juvenile, General Reference, Academic Reference
Paulist Press is an ecumenical publisher with Roman Catholic roots. We publish academic and pastoral theology, Roman Catholic studies, and books on scripture, liturgy, spirituality, church history, philosophy, and religion and public affairs. Our publishing is oriented toward adult non-fiction, with the exception of a few books for children. We do not publish poetry or fiction.
Acquisitions focus for 1998-9: No special focus for the immediate future beyond the best contemporary treatments of our overall publishing program.
In print: 1200 titles.   1997: 100 titles.
3% of titles author-subsidized
ISBN Prefix(es): 0-8091

Recent/Forthcoming Titles: Vincent Branick, *The New Testament: An Introduction*; Maureen Gallaher, *The Art of Cathechesis*; Frank Tobin (trans. & intro.), *Mechthild of Magedeburg: The Flowing Light of the Godhead* (in the Classics of Western Spirituality series)
Manuscript guidelines free upon request
Preferred form of initial contact: Proposal package containing SASE, outline, and 2-3 sample chapters.
Send submissions to—
    All adult nonfiction: Donald Brophy, Managing Editor
    Children's books: Karen Scialabba

111   Penn State University Press
Subsidiary/division of The Pennsylvania State University
USB #1, Suite C, 820 N University Dr, University Park, PA 16802-1003
Phone: 814-865-1327
Fax: 814-863-1408
E-mail: PXW3@psu.edu
Subject areas: Ethics, Comparative Religions, History of Religion(s), Mythology, Sacred Languages, Philosophy of Religion, Religion and Art, Religion and Literature, Religion and Cultural/Ethnic Studies, Religion and Gender Studies, Sacred Literature — Commentary & Hermeneutics, Biblical Literature — Translations, Sacred Literature — Philology & Linguistics, Sacred Literature — Cultural & Historical Contexts, Tantric/Vedic Lit. — Translations, Buddhist Literature — Translations
Types of publications: Translations, Scholarly Monographs
Our program concentrates on books of importance for scholars; our fields include history, philosophy, Biblical studies, literature, theology, and art history. We have two series: "Hermeneutics: Studies in the History of Religions" and the "Penn State Series in Lived Religious Experience."
In print: 65 titles.   1997: 4 titles.
ISBN Prefix(es): 0-271
Recent/Forthcoming Titles: Lee Hoinacki, *El Camino: Walking to Santiago de Compostella*; Jess Hollenbach, *Mysticism: Experience, Response, and Empowerment*; Rachel Brenner, *Writing as Resistance: Four Women Confronting the Holocaust: Edith Stein, Simone Weil, Anne Frank, Etty Hillesum*

No manuscript guidelines available
Preferred form of initial contact: Short written query
Send submissions to—
  Philip Winsor, Senior Editor

112   Peter Lang Publishing, Inc
Subsidiary/division of Verlag Peter Lang AG (Switz.)
275 7th Ave, 28th Floor, New York, NY 10001
Phone: 212-647-7700, 800-770-5264 (Cust. Svc.)
Fax: 212-647-7707
WWW homepage: www.peterlang.com
Subject areas: Religious Thought/Theology, Religious Studies, Religion and Society, Sacred Literature
Types of publications: Classroom Instructional Materials, Essay/ Lecture Collections, Scholarly Monographs, Dissertations
Acquisitions focus for 1998-9: Monographs and textbooks in the specified areas.
In print: 200 titles.   1997: 30 titles.
 90% of titles author-subsidized
ISBN Prefix(es): 0-8204
Recent/Forthcoming Titles: Winston Arthur Lawson, *Religion and Race*; David H. Turner, *Return to Eden*; Dennis R. Creswell, *St. Augustine's Dilemma*
Manuscript guidelines free upon request
Preferred form of initial contact: Short written query
Send submissions to—
  Owen Lancer, Acquisitions Editor

113   Pickwick Publications
4137 Timberlane Drive, Allison Park, PA 15101
Fax: 412-487-8862
E-mail: DYH1@aol.com
Subject areas: Liturgy and Ritual, Preaching & Homiletics, Religious Biography, Ethics, Doctrinal Theology & Dogma, Systematic Theology, Sacred Literature — Commentary & Hermeneutics, Sacred Literature — Philology & Linguistics

Types of publications: Classroom Instructional Materials, Essay/Lecture Collections, Reprints, Translations, Poetry, Scholarly Monographs, Dissertations, General Reference
In print: 105 titles.
ISBN Prefix(es): 0-915138, 1-55635
Recent/Forthcoming Titles: Philip R. Throne, *Evangelism and Karl Barth*; C. K. Barrett, *Jesus and the Word and Other Essays*; Rudolf Pesch, *The Trial of Jesus Continues*
No manuscript guidelines available
Preferred form of initial contact: Proposal package containing SASE, outline, and 1 sample chapter.

114   The Pilgrim Press
Subsidiary/division of United Church Board for Homeland Ministries
700 Prospect Ave E, Cleveland, OH 44115-1100
Phone: 216-736-3715, 800-654-5129 (orders)
Fax: 216-736-3703, 216-736-3713 (orders)
WWW homepage: www.pilgrimpress.com
Publisher: Lynne Deming, Ph.D.
Subject areas: Liturgy and Ritual, Prayer & Meditation, Ethics, Systematic Theology, Pluralistic/Ecumenical Theology, Religion and Gender Studies, Religion and the Physical Sciences, Religion and the Natural Sciences, Religion and Law, Religion and Public Policy
Types of publications: Classroom Instructional Materials, Music, Essay/Lecture Collections, Devotional Guides, Self-Help, Scholarly Monographs, Academic Reference
Pilgrim Press focuses on 1) ethics and theology (including science, technology, and medicine); 2) human identity and relationships (including gay/lesbian/bisexual/transgendered; men's studies; and women's studies); and 3) activist spirituality.
In print: 300 titles.   1997: 30 titles.   ISBN Prefix(es): 0-8298
Recent/Forthcoming Titles: *Ritualizing Women: Patterns of Spirituality*; *Sexuality: A Reader*; *The Humanzing Brain: Where Religion and Neuroscience Meet*
Manuscript guidelines free upon request
Preferred form of initial contact: Proposal package containing short written query, SASE, outline, 1 sample chapter, and author's C.V.
Send submissions to—
    Timothy G. Staveteig, Editor
Limitations/Restrictions: No material returned without SASE.

115   Princeton University Press
41 William St, Princeton, NJ 08540
Phone: 609-258-4900, 800-777-4726 (orders), 609-883-1759 (orders)
Fax: 609-258-6305, 800-999-1958 (orders)
E-mail: admalmud@pupress.princeton.edu
WWW homepage: pup.pupress.princeton.edu (info & orders)
Subject areas: Philosophy of Religion, Religion and Art, Religion and
    Literature, Religion and Classics, Religion and Cultural/Ethnic
    Studies, Religion and Gender Studies, Sociology of Religion,
    Anthropology of Religion, Religion in Popular Culture/Media,
    Sacred Literature — Translations
Types of publications: Classroom Instructional Materials, Illustrated
    Books, Essay/Lecture Collections, Translations, Scholarly
    Monographs, Dissertations, General Reference
Princeton University Press publishes scholarship devoted to American
    religion, Asian religions, late antiquity, Jewish studies, and the
    cultural study of religion.
In print: 338 titles.   1997: 31 title.
ISBN Prefix(es): 0-691
Recent/Forthcoming Titles: David Hall, ed., *Lived Religion in America*;
    Rodney Stark, *The Rise of Christianity*; Russell, *A History of Heaven*
No manuscript guidelines available
Preferred form of initial contact: Short written query
Send submissions to—
    Religion/Asian Studies: A. D. Malmud, Editor

116   Publishers Associates
PO Box 140361, Irving (Las Colinas Business Park), TX 75104-0361
Phone: 972-681-9190
Fax: 972-686-5332
WWW homepage: www.idehouse.com
Chief Operating Officer: Dr. Belinda Buxjom
CEO: Dr. Jefferson Stryker
Dir. Mss.: Dr. Rick Donovon
Subject areas: Religious Life/Practice, Religious Thought/Theology,
    Religious Studies, Religion and Society, Sacred Literature, Religious
    Education
Types of publications: Scholarly Monographs, Dissertations

Publishers Associates publishes works devoted to all issues of all faiths. Our member presses include The Liberal Press, Liberal Arts Press, Monument Press, and Tangelwuld Press. All our publications are gender-neutral and nonsexist.
In print: 200 titles.   1997: 50 titles.
ISBN Prefix(es): 0-9308383, 0-934667, 0-935175
Recent/Forthcoming Titles: *Angels in August*; *Religion in Ancient Arabia*; *The Hindu Faith*
Send #10 SASE for MS guidelines
Preferred form of initial contact: Proposal package containing SASE, outline, and author's academic vitae.
Send submissions to—
Belinda Buxjom, COO
Limitations/Restrictions: No sexism unless it is the subject of work. We don't publish polemics, works that are demeaning to women, homophobic, xenophobic, or diminish any person or group.
Submissions must include full footnotes and bibliography.

117   Ragged Edge Press
Subsidiary/division of White Mane Publishing Company
63 W Bund Street, PO Box 152, Shippenburg, PA 17257
Phone: 717-532-2237
Fax: 717-532-7704
Cust. Svc. Manager: Tammy Garmen
Marketing Assistant: Lorin Morris
Faith/denominational/cultural focus: Christian
Subject areas: Liturgy and Ritual, Prayer & Meditation, Spiritual Life/Personal Religion, Religious Biography, Theological Education (methodology), History of Religion(s), Religion and Music, Psychology of Religion, Sociology of Religion, Biblical Literature — Cultural & Historical Contexts, Biblical Literature — Translations, Religious Education — Elementary, Religious Education — Seminary, Religious Education — Adult
Types of publications: Devotional Guides, Self-Help, Fiction — Juvenile (historically-based), General Reference, Academic Reference
Ragged Edge Press was formed with the intention of making a difference in people's lives by using God and Biblically-based themes

to attempt to aid people in seeing and understanding God as well as living lives with the presence of God.

Acquisitions focus for 1998-9: Major themes include Christian marriage and marriage improvement, along with titles to aid in exploring God from a vision of God and Nature to a prayer style of God's questions.

In print: 8 titles. 1997: 3 titles.

10% of titles author-subsidized

ISBN Prefix(es): 1-57249, 0-942597

Recent/Forthcoming Titles: Paul G. Johnson, *God and World Religions*; Browne Barr, *Never Too Late to be Loved*; Callen I. K. Story, *The Everlasting Song: The Book of John*

Manuscript guidelines free upon request

Preferred form of initial contact: Proposal package containing SASE, outline, and 2 sample chapters (send for guidelines first).

Send submissions to—

Harold Collins, Acquisitions Editor

Acquisitions address: 353 Ragged Edge Road, Chambersburg, PA 17201

118   Rainbow Books (California)

Imprint of Rainbow Publishers

PO Box 261129, San Diego, CA 92196

Street Address: 9230 Trade Place, San Diego, CA 92126

Phone: 619-271-7600

Faith/denominational/cultural focus: Evangelical Christian

Subject areas: Religious Education — Elementary and Secondary

Types of publications: Classroom Instructional Materials

We publish reproducible books for teachers of children in the Christian classroom (church, Christian school or home school). These books are 64-128 pages in length and are issued in age/grade levels. Themes include activities, lessons, crafts, puzzles, and games. Our books are Bible-based and teacher-friendly. We also publish teacher aids such as bulletin board books.

Acquisitions focus for 1998-9: Innovative puzzles, games (especially for 5th and 6th graders), new treatments of Bible stories with creative activities.

In print: 150 titles.   1997: 8 titles.

Recent/Forthcoming Titles: *Make and Learn Bible Toys*; *Instant Bible Lessons*; *Interactive Bible Bulletin Boards*

Send SASE for manuscript guidelines
Preferred form of initial contact: Proposal package containing SASE,
   outline, 2-5 sample chapters, and author biography.
Send submissions to—Christy Allen, Editor
Research what is available in Christian bookstores before submitting
   manuscript; then tell us how your book fills a need in the market.

119   Rainbow Books, Inc (Florida)
PO Box 430, Highland City, FL 33846-0430
Phone: 941-648-4420, 800-356-9315 (Visa, MC, AMEX orders)
Fax: 941-648-4420
E-mail: naip@aol.com
Publisher: Betty Wright
Senior Editor: Betsy Lampe
Production Manager: Virginia Condello
Chief Accountant: Carl Fedele
Asst. to Publisher: Charles M. Lampe
Marketing Asst.: Jamie Peters
Production Manager: Marilyn Razlaff
Foreign Rights: GAIA MEDIA/Switzerland
Faith/denominational/cultural focus: Christian (liberal)
Subject areas: Religious Life/Practice (in contemporary culture),
   Religion and Society
Types of publications: How-To
We want to provide information that solves problems encountered in
   today's culture in a kinder, gentler fashion, religiously oriented.
Acquisitions focus for 1998-9: We are particularly interested in
   nonfiction how-to books that show people how to live in today's
   culture.
In print: 4 titles. 1997: 4 titles.
ISBN Prefix(es): 1-56825
Recent/Forthcoming Titles: Barbara Jackson, *Rx for Christianity*; Albert
   Wells, *Strong is the Peace*
Send #10 SASE for manuscript guidelines
Preferred form of initial contact: Proposal package containing SASE
   and complete manuscript — no partials
Send submissions to—
   Betsy Lampe, Senior Editor
Limitations/Restrictions: No manuscripts touting the religious right.
Please request guidelines first, then take those guidelines to heart.

120   Religious Education Press
5316 Meadow Brook Road, Birmingham, AL 35242-3315
Phone: 205-991-1000 (8 am - 5 pm Central)
Fax: 205-991-9669
E-mail: releduc@ix.netcom.com
WWW homepage: www.bham.net/releduc
Publisher: James Michael Lee
VP, Operations: Nancy J. Vickers
Faith/denominational/cultural focus: Ecumenical Christian
Subject areas: Pastoral Theology, Theological Ed. (Methodology), Psychology of Religion, Religious Education
Types of publications: Classroom Instructional Materials, Scholarly Monographs
Religious Education Press publishes serious, scholarly books in the field of religious education for an ecumenical audience. Our books are used by professionals in the field, and are also used in academic settings in colleges, universities, and seminaries as textbooks as well as in libraries. Our publishing program also covers areas closely related to religious education, including pastoral theology, religious psychology, and moral development.
In print: 65 titles.   1997: 3 titles.
ISBN Prefix(es): 0-89135
Recent/Forthcoming Titles: Harley Atkinson, *Ministry with Youth in Crisis*; Barbara Wilkerson, *Multicultural Religious Education*; Nancy T. Foltz, ed., *Handbook of Planning in Religious Education*
Send SASE for manuscript guidelines
Preferred form of initial contact: Proposal package containing SASE, outline, and 1 sample chapter.
Send submissions to—
    Dr. Nancy J. Vickers, VP, Operations
Please describe your expertise for writing and include sufficient return postage for your materials should we decide not to publish them.

121   Fleming H. Revell
Subsidiary/division of Baker Book House Co
PO Box 6287, Grand Rapids, MI 49516-6287
Phone: 616-676-9185
Fax: 616-676-2315
WWW homepage: www.bakerbooks.com

President: Dwight Baker
Dir. of Publications: Allan Fisher
Faith/denominational/cultural focus: Protestant
Subject areas: Prayer & Meditation, Spiritual Life/Personal Religion, Religion and the Family, Religion and Health, Comparative Religions, Religion in Popular Culture/Media
Types of publications: Books-on-Tape, Illustrated Books, Reprints, Devotional Guides, General Interest Nonfiction — Adult, Fiction — Adult, Self-Help
Acquisitions focus for 1998-9: Popular manuscripts that touch the heart of the reader.
1997: 50 titles.
Recent/Forthcoming Titles: Robert A. Schuller, *In Search of Morality*; Karen Linamen, *Pillow Talk*; Jane Peart, *Perilous Bargain*
Manuscript guidelines available on web site.
Preferred form of initial contact: Proposal package containing SASE, outline, and 2-3 sample chapters.
Send submissions to—
   Linda Holland, Editorial Director
Bill Petersen, Senior Editor
Limitations/Restrictions: No e-mail or phone queries accepted. Allow at least 90 days for response.

122   Routledge
29 West 35th Street, New York, NY 10001
U.K./European Acquisitions: Adrian Driscoll, Routledge, 11 New Fetter Lane, London EC4P 4EE United Kingdom
Phone: 212-244-3336
Fax: 212-563-2269
Subject areas: Religious Studies, Religion and Society
Types of publications: Essay/Lecture Collections, General Interest Nonfiction — Adult, Scholarly Monographs
Routledge publishes a broad range of titles: religion in society, studies of religion and religious movements, connections between religion and other fields (anthropology, sociology, gender studies, science, popular culture, history, race studies, politics). Our primary focus is books, but journal ideas are also welcome. Level: scholarly trade, course adoption, general interest.

Acquisitions focus for 1998-9: Religion and American life; women and religion/gender and religion; religion and popular culture.

ISBN Prefix(es): 415-9

Manuscript guidelines free upon request

Preferred form of initial contact: Proposal package containing letter of inquiry, 1-2 page proposal, and author's C.V.

Send submissions to—

William P. Germano, VP and Publications Director

123   Rudra Press

Subsidiary/division of Productivity Press

PO Box 13390, Portland, OR 97213

Street Address: 541 NE 20th Ave, Suite 108, Portland, OR 97232

Phone: 503-235-0175, 800-786-7798 (orders)

Fax: 503-235-0909

E-mail: lorraine@rudra.com

WWW homepage: www.rudra.com

President: Karen Kreiger

Senior Editor: Cheryl Rosen

Cust. Svc. Manager: Lorraine Millard

Managing Editor: Ellen Hynson

Marketing Manager: Sarah Fahey

Faith/denominational/cultural focus: Spirituality

Subject areas: Prayer & Meditation, Spiritual Life/Personal Religion, Religion and Health, Religious Biography, Comparative Religions, History of Religion(s), Mythology, Sacred Languages, Interdisciplinary Studies, Sacred Literature

Types of publications: Audio-Visual, Music, Illustrated Books, Essay/Lecture Collections, Reprints, Translations, Self-Help, Poetry, General Reference

Rudra Press publishes books, audios and videos on spiritual life, meditation, eastern philosophy, yoga, sound and healing, and alternative medicine.

Acquisitions focus for 1998-9: Spirituality, healing with sound and music, meditation, and eastern philosophy.

In print: 35 titles.   1997: 6 titles.

ISBN Prefix(es): 0-915801

Recent/Forthcoming Titles: *Meditation*; *The Breath of God*; *Will I Be the Hero of My Own Life?*

Send SASE for manuscript guidelines
Preferred form of initial contact: Proposal package containing SASE, outline, and 2-3 sample chapters.
Send submissions to—
Ellen Hynson, Managing Editor
Include information on previously published works, lectures, media appearances, intended audience, and competitive works.

124   Rutgers University Press
Subsidiary/division of Rutgers University
PO Box 5062, New Brunswick, NJ 08903
Street Address: Building 4161, Livingston Campus, Joyce Kilmer Ave/Rockerfeller Rd, Piscataway, NJ 08854
Phone: 732-445-7762, 800-446-9323 (orders)
Fax: 732-445-7039
E-mail: woodley@rci.rutgers.edu
WWW homepage: rutgerspress.rutgers.edu
Director: Marlie Wasserman
Faith/denominational/cultural focus: All faiths with emphasis on Judaism
Subject areas: History of Religion(s), Religion and Music, Religion and Cultural/Ethnic Studies, Sociology of Religion, Anthropology of Religion, Religion and Society
Types of publications: Classroom Instructional Materials, Illustrated Books, General Interest Nonfiction — Adult, General Reference, Academic Reference
We publish accessible, well-written academic and general interest books on the social and cultural study of religion. We are particularly interested in the intersection between ethnicity and religion, gender and religion, and sexuality and religion. Our list in Jewish studies is especially dynamic.
In print: 40 titles.   1997: 15 titles.
ISBN Prefix(es): 0-8135
Recent/Forthcoming Titles: David Shallenberger, *Reclaiming the Spirit: Gay Men and Lesbians Come to Terms with Religion*; Nancy Ammerman, *Congregation and Community*; Norman Kleeblatt, ed., *Too Jewish? Challenging Traditional Identities*
Manuscript guidelines free upon request

Preferred form of initial contact: Proposal package containing SASE, outline, 2 sample chapters, author's CV, and paragraph describing intended market/audience
Send submissions to—
Martha Heller, Acquisitions Editor

125   William H Sadlier, Inc
Subsidiary/division of Sadlier
9 Pine Street, New York, NY 10005
Phone: 212-227-2120, 800-221-5175 (customer service)
Fax: 212-267-8696, 212-312-6080 (customer service)
WWW homepage: www.sadlier.com
Chairman of the Board: Frank Sadlier Dinger
President: William Sadlier Dinger
Executive VP & Publisher: Dr. Gerard F. Baumbach
VP, Treasurer: Henry E. Christel
VP, Editor-in-Chief: Moya Gullage
National Sales Manager: Gregory Schweiker
National Field Sales Man.: John Bonenberger
Faith/denominational/cultural focus: Roman Catholic
Subject areas: Prayer & Meditation, Religious Education — Elementary, Religious Education — Secondary, Religious Education — Adult, Catechetical
Types of publications: Classroom Instructional Materials, Audio-Visual
We publish religion series textbooks, guides and components for Catholic school and parish catechetical programs for elementary and junior high age children and young people. Various other catechetical materials are published for youth and adult enrichment. Some of these materials are produced on cassettes and video tapes.
Acquisitions focus for 1998-9: Catechetical materials for children, families, and adults; liturgical catechesis materials.
ISBN Prefix(es): 0-8215
Recent/Forthcoming Titles: COMING TO FAITH Program, KEYSTONE Edition, K-6 for Parish and Catholic School Programs; FAITH AND WITNESS Program 7-8, 5 Courses for Parish and Catholic Schools; SADLIER SACRAMENT Program
MS guidelines available after proposal acceptance.
Preferred form of initial contact: Short written query
Send submissions to—
Dr. Gerard F. Baumbach, Publisher

126   St Anthony Messenger Press and Franciscan Communications
1615 Republic Street, Cincinnati, OH 45210-1298
Phone: 513-241-5615, 800-488-0488 (orders)
Fax: 513-241-1197, 513-241-0399 (orders)
E-mail: StAnthony@AmericanCatholic.org
WWW homepage: www.AmericanCatholic.org
President: John Bok, OFM
Publisher: Jeremy Harrington, OFM
Editor-in-Chief: Norman Perry, OFM
Business Manager: Thomas Shumate
Managing Editor: Lisa Biedenbach
Director of Marketing: Tom Bruce
Asst. Dir. of Marketing: Barbara Baker
National Sales Representative: John Koize
Permissions Manager: Margaret Warminski
Faith/denominational/cultural focus: Roman Catholic
Subject areas: Liturgy and Ritual, Prayer & Meditation, Preaching & Homiletics, Spiritual Life/Personal Religion, Religion and the Family, Ethics, Doctrinal Theology & Dogma, Pastoral Theology, Religion in Popular Culture/Media, Religious Education — Elementary, Religious Education — Secondary, Religious Education — Adult
Types of publications: Classroom Instructional Materials, Audio-Visual, Illustrated Books, Devotional Guides, Liturgical Materials, General Interest Nonfiction — Adult, General Interest Nonfiction — Juvenile
Our press seeks to spread the Word that is Jesus Christ in the style of Saints Francis and Anthony. Through print and electronic media marketed in North America and worldwide, we endeavor to evangelize, inspire and inform those who search for God and seek a richer Catholic, Christian, human life. Our efforts help support the life, ministry, and charities of the Franciscan Friars of St. John the Baptist Province who sponsor our work. We publish a national Catholic family magazine (Circ. 350,000+); monthly newsletters for adult and teen Catholics on particular topics; a scripture monthly newsletter; 2 homily services; books; audios and videos. Subject areas include Catholic identity and Church history, scripture, Fransicana, resources for parish ministry, sacraments and liturgy, and prayer and spirituality. We publish some children's materials.
Acquisitions focus for 1998-9: Scripture, Catholic identity, and prayer and spirituality.

In print: 100 titles.   1997: 40 titles.
ISBN Prefix(es): 0-86716
Recent/Forthcoming Titles: *Called to Preside: A Handbook for Lay Presiders; A Retreat with Our Lady, Dominic and Ignatius: Praying with Our Bodies; Reading the Gospels with the Church: From Christmas through Easter*
Manuscript guidelines free upon request
Preferred form of initial contact: Short written query
Send submissions to—
    Lisa Biedenbach, Managing Editor
Limitations/Restrictions: No simultaneous submissions.
Make sure material is suited for our market and fits our niche (request catalog and guidelines).

127   Saint Joseph's University Press
5600 City Ave, Philadelphia, PA 19131-1395
Phone: 610-660-3400
Fax: 610-660-3410
E-mail: ccroce@sju.edu
Editorial Director: Rev. Joseph F. Chorpenning, OSFS
Faith/denominational/cultural focus: Roman Catholic
Subject areas: Folklore, Religion and Art, Religion and Literature, Religion and Cultural/Ethnic Studies, Religion in Popular Culture/Media, Biblical Literature — Cultural & Historical Contexts
Types of publications: Illustrated Books, Essay/Lecture Collections, Devotional Guides, Scholarly Monographs, General Reference, Academic Reference
Saint Joseph's University Press focuses primarily on Spanish American Colonial art and iconography. It also publishes essays, lectures, and talks on the saints and their place in the arts.
In print: 13 titles.   1997: 3 titles.
ISBN Prefix(es): 0-916101
Recent/Forthcoming Titles: *A Man to Heal Differences: Essays and Talks on St. Francis de Sales; The Holy Family in Art and Devotion; St. Joseph in Matthew's Gospel*
No manuscript guidelines available
No unsolicited submissions accepted

128   St. Martin's Press, Inc
175 5th Ave, New York, NY 10010
Phone: 212-674-5151, 212-982-3900 (x268)
E-mail: michaelflamini@stmartins.com
Subject areas: Religious Studies, Religion and Society
Types of publications: Essay/Lecture Collections, General Interest Nonfiction — Adult (Trade), General Interest Nonfiction — Adult (Trade Biography), Scholarly Monographs, General Reference
Our publishing program centers around an interest in the role of religion in society and culture.
Acquisitions focus for 1998-9: A mixture of both scholarly and trade non-fiction books.
In print: 300 titles.   1997: 25 titles.
ISBN Prefix(es): 0-312
Recent/Forthcoming Titles: Donald Wiebe, *The Politics of Religious Studies*; Jon Stone, *On the Boundaries of American Evangelism*; Justin Watson, *The Christian Coalition*
No manuscript guidelines available
Preferred form of initial contact: Proposal package containing SASE, outline, and at least 1 sample chapter.
Send submissions to—
    Michael J. Flamini, Senior Editor
    Karen Wolny, Editor
    Maura Burnett, Assistant Editor
Send submissions to "Scholarly & Reference Division" at HQ address.

129   St Nectarios Press
10300 Ashworth Ave North, Seattle, WA 98133-9410
Phone: 206-522-4471, 800-643-4233 (orders)
Fax: 206-523-0550
E-mail: books@orthodoxpress.org
WWW homepage: www.orthodoxpress.org
Director: Rev. Neketas S. Palassis
Faith/denominational/cultural focus: Eastern Orthodox
Subject areas: Liturgy and Ritual, Spiritual Life/Personal Religion, Religion and the Family, Hagiography, Doctrinal Theology & Dogma, Ecumenical Theology, Biblical Literature — Translations

Types of publications: Music, Illustrated Books, Essay/Lecture Collections, Reprints, Liturgical Materials, General Interest Nonfiction — Adult, General Interest Nonfiction — Juvenile, Translations, Scholarly Monographs

Materials devoted to the study and practice of traditional Eastern Orthodox Christianity. Our emphasis is on hagiography and devotional materials.

In print: 27 titles.   1997: 4 titles.

ISBN Prefix(es): 0-913026

Recent/Forthcoming Titles: *Saints of Anglo-Saxon England, vol. 3; Pilgrim's Guide to the Holy Land for Orthodox Christians; The Life of St. Barbara the Great Martyr*

No manuscript guidelines available

Preferred form of initial contact: Short written query

Limitations/Restrictions: Eastern Orthodox Christianity only.

130   Scepter Publishers

PO Box 1270, Princeton, NJ 08542

Phone: 609-683-8773

Fax: 609-683-8780

WWW homepage: scepterpub.org

Faith/denominational/cultural focus: Roman Catholic

Subject areas: Liturgy and Ritual, Prayer & Meditation, Vocational/Pastoral Guidance, Spiritual Life/Personal Religion, Religion and the Family, Religious Biography, Doctrinal Theology

Types of publications: Books-on-Tape, Reprints, General Interest Nonfiction — Adult

Scepter primarily publishes books focusing on Catholic teaching in family life, education, prayer, Bible study and liturgy.

In print: 45 titles.   1997: 12 titles.

Manuscript guidelines free upon request

Preferred form of initial contact: Short written query

131   Scholars Press
PO Box 15399, Atlanta, GA 30333-0399
Street: 825 Houston Mill Rd, Atlanta, GA 30329
Phone: 404-727-2320, 888-747-2354 (toll free orders),
    404-727-2354 (direct dial orders)
Fax: 404-727-2348
E-mail: scholar@emory.edu
WWW homepage: scholar.cc.emory.edu
Director: Harry W. Gilmer
Associate Director: Dennis Ford
Editorial Director: Rex Matthews
Publications Manager: Theodore Brelsford
Subject areas: Religious Thought/Theology, Religious Studies, Religion and Society, Sacred Literature, Religious Education — Seminary
Types of publications: Classroom Instructional Materials, Electronic Publications (CD-ROM & Internet), Essay/Lecture Collections, Reprints, Translations, Scholarly Monographs, Dissertations, Language Reference, Academic Reference
Scholars Press publishes on behalf of a consortium of 21 organizations, including the American Academy of Religion, the Society for Biblical Literature, and the American Schools of Oriental Research. Its primary focus is the publication of academically informed works on religion, biblical studies, and related areas, intended for professional-level students and instructors, and college and university libraries. The program includes translations of texts from the ancient Near East, dissertations, academic monographs, collections, Festschrifts, and works addressing a broader audience outside the academy. Additional information about Scholars Press and a complete listing of titles is available on the Internet at http://scholar.cc.emory.edu.
Acquisitions focus for 1998-9: Academically informed, non-sectarian works that interpret religion's meaning and relevance to a broader public, including creative approaches to biblical texts and their historical and cultural settings.
In print: 1400 titles.   1997: 90 titles.
ISBN Prefix(es): 1-55540, 0-7885, 0-89130
Recent/Forthcoming Titles: Richard Penaskovic, *Critical Thinking and the Academic Study of Religion*; J. Samuel Preus, *Explaining Religion: Criticism & Theory from Bodin to Freud*; Odil H. Steck, *Old Testament Exegesis: A Guide to the Methodology*
No manuscript guidelines available

Preferred form of initial contact: Short written query
Send submissions to—
   Rex Matthews, Editorial Director
Limitations: Submissions must be non-sectarian & non-fictional.

132   Science & Behavior Books
PO Box 60519, Palo Alto, CA 94306
Phone: 415-965-0954
Fax: 415-965-8998
E-mail: SBBKS@aol.com
WWW homepage: users.aol.com/sbbks/index.com
Faith/denominational/cultural focus: Christian
Subject areas: Spiritual Life/Personal Religion, Religion and the
   Family, Pastoral Theology, Psychology of Religion
Types of publications: General Interest Nonfiction — Adult, Self-Help
In print: 1 title.
ISBN Prefix(es): 0-8314
Send SASE for manuscript guidelines
Preferred form of initial contact: Proposal package containing outline
   or sample chapters
Send submissions to—
   Robert S. Spitzer, Editor-in-Chief

133   SeedSowers Publishing House
PO Box 285, Sargent, GA 30275
Phone: 770-254-9442
Fax: 770-254-1024
E-mail: seedsowers@mindspring.com
WWW homepage: www.clayactive.com/seedsowers
Vice President: Gene Edwards
Faith/denominational/cultural focus: Christian
Subject areas: Liturgy and Ritual, Prayer & Meditation, Vocational/
   Pastoral Guidance, Missions, Spiritual Life/Personal Religion,
   House Church Movement, Doctrinal Theology & Dogma, Pastoral

Theology, Theological Education (methodology), Biblical Literature — Cultural & Historical Contexts

Types of publications: Books-on-Tape, Devotional Guides, General Interest Nonfiction — Adult, Self-Help, General Reference

We specialize in two streams: 1) the Deeper Christian Life Books on prayer and fellowship with the Lord; and 2) the House Church movement: books and tapes on meeting in homes rather than the traditional church setting (includes practical and historical).

In print: 55 titles.   1997: 4 titles.

ISBN Prefix(es): 0-940232

Recent/Forthcoming Titles: *Overlooked Christianity*; *Centrality of Jesus Christ*; *Bone of His Bone*

No manuscript guidelines available

No unsolicited submissions accepted

134   Sepher-Hermon Press, Inc

1265 46th Street, Brooklyn, NY 11219

Phone: 718-972-9010

Fax: 718-972-9010

Faith/denominational/cultural focus: Judaism

Subject areas: Religious Bio., Ethics, Talmudic Lit. — Translations

Types of publications: Reprints, Translations, Scholarly Monographs

In print: 50 titles.   1997: 5 titles.   ISBN Prefix(es): 0-87203

35% of titles author-subsidized

Recent/Forthcoming Titles: Dr. Gloria Pollack, *Jewish Festivals*

No manuscript guidelines available

Preferred form of initial contact: Short written query

Send submissions to—

Samuel Gross, President

135   Shambhala Publications Inc
PO Box 308, Back Bay Annex, Boston, MA 02117-0308
Orders: Random House Order Department, 400 Hahn Rd, Westminster, MD 21157-9939
Phone: 617-424-0030, 800-733-3000 (orders)
Fax: 617-236-1563, 800-793-2665 (orders)
E-mail: editors@shambhala.com
WWW homepage: www.shambhala.com
Faith/denominational/cultural focus: Multicultural philosophy & spirituality from Buddhism, Zen and Taoism to Kabbalah, Hindu studies, and Christian mystics.
Subject areas: Spiritual Life/Personal Religion, Religion and Health, Religious Biography, Comparative Religions, History of Religion(s), Mythology, Philosophy of Religion, Religion and Art, Religion and Music, Buddhist Literature — Translations
Types of publications: Books-on-Tape, Illustrated Books, Essay/Lecture Collections, Reprints, General Interest Nonfiction — Adult, Fiction — Adult, Translations, Self-Help, Poetry, General Reference
Shambhala publishes books of quality that express the potential of inner evolution and the values and aspirations of individuals and society, with special interest in philosophy, religion, art, literature, cultural studies, psychology, health, and global concerns.
In print: 250 titles.   1997: 60 titles.
ISBN Prefix(es): 0-87773; 1-57062
Recent/Forthcoming Titles: *The Secret of Francis of Assisi*; Sharon Salzberg, *A Heart as Wide as the World*; Ursula K. LeGuin (trans.), *Lao Tzu: Tao Teh Ching*
Manuscript guidelines free upon request
Preferred form of initial contact: Short written query or proposal package containing SASE, outline, at least 2 sample chapters, table of contents, and author C.V. or résumé.
Send submissions to—
Peter Turner, Senior Editor
Limitations/Restrictions: No children's' books.
Please expect response in 4 to 6 weeks from date of receipt.

136   M E Sharpe, Inc, Publisher
80 Business Park Drive, Armonk, NY 10504
Phone: 914-273-1800, 800-541-6563 (orders)
Fax: 914-273-2106
Subject areas: Ethics, Comparative Religions, History of Religion(s), Philosophy of Religion, Religion and Art, Religion and Literature, Religion and Cultural/Ethnic Studies, Religion and Gender Studies, Sociology of Religion, Anthropology of Religion, Religion and Political Science, Religion and Society, Religion in Popular Culture/Media, Religion and Public Policy, Koranic Literature — Commentary & Hermeneutics
Types of publications: Classroom Instructional Materials, Essay/Lecture Collections, General Interest Nonfiction — Adult, Scholarly Monographs, General Reference, Academic Reference
M. E. Sharpe is a social science book and journal publisher. We have been, up until recently, a publisher of scholarly and academic books in economics, political science, and history, with fuller development in certain area studies (Asia, Russia, and Latin America in particular). Many of our books sell in paperback as ancillary texts for college courses. Two years ago we inaugurated a list in religion, acquiring books across a range of markets: core textbooks, secondary texts, academic trade titles, and some scholarly monographs. In 1996, Charles Lippy (University of Tennessee-Chattanooga) became the general editor of our new series "Religion in American Culture and Society." By the end of 1997, we will have 8 religion titles in print, with plans to aggressively increase that number.
Acquisitions focus for 1998-9: Core textbooks in comparative and/or world religions; mainstream undergraduate texts in ethics; other topical areas relating to American culture.
In print: 8 titles. 1997: 8 titles.
Recent/Forthcoming Titles: P. Vardy and M. Mills, *The Puzzle of the Gospels*; P. Vardy, *The Puzzle of Ethics*; D. Swift, *Religion and the American Experience: A Social and Cultural History, 1756-1996*
Manuscript guidelines free upon request
Preferred form of initial contact: Proposal package containing outline, sample chapters, C.V. or resume, proposed market for the book (this may include description of similar books already published); overall length of manuscript and rough deadline for completion (if not complete)
Send submissions to—
Religious Studies: Executive Editor, Peter Coveney

137   Harold Shaw Publishers

388 Gunderson, Box 567, Wheaton, IL 60819
Phone: 630-665-6700
Fax: 630-655-6793
E-mail: Shawpub@compuserve.com
Editorial Director: Joan Guest
Publisher: Stephen Board
Faith/denominational/cultural focus: Evangelical Christian
Subject areas: Prayer & Meditation, Missions, Spiritual Life/Personal
    Religion, Religion and the Family, Religion and Health, Religious
    Biography, Inspirational Gift Books, Religion and Art, Religion and
    Literature, Psychology of Religion, Religion in Popular
    Culture/Media
Types of publications: Reprints, Devotional Guides, General Interest
    Nonfiction — Adult, Fiction — Adult (1-2 per year only), Self-Help,
    Poetry (1-2 per year only)
Harold Shaw Publishers publish books for practical Christian living and
    the literary-minded reader. We avoid sensational or highly sectarian
    topics.
Acquisitions focus for 1998-9: We consider any well-written book that
    meets a need among Christian people and is from an evangelical
    world-view.
In print: 300 titles.   1997: 38 titles.
ISBN Prefix(es): 0-87788
Recent/Forthcoming Titles: Elaine McEwan, *Managing Attention and
    Learning Disorders*; Madeleine L'Engle, *Bright Evening Star*; Dr.
    Grace Ketterman, *Ketterman on Kids: Answers to Questions Parents
    Ask Most*
Manuscript guidelines free upon request; send 9 x 12" SASE (5 stamps)
    for catalog.
Preferred form of initial contact: Proposal package containing SASE,
    outline, and 1-3 sample chapters.
Send submissions to—
    Christian self-help/nonfiction: Joan Guest, Editorial Director
    Literary works: Lil Copan, Editor
    Bible study guides: Mary Horner Collins, Editor
Limitations: No simultaneous submissions. Do not fax queries.

138   Sheed & Ward
Subsidiary/division of The National Catholic Reporter
115 E Armour Blvd, PO Box 419492, Kansas City, MO 64141-6492
Phone: 816-531-0538, 800-333-7373 (Customer Service), 800-444-8910 (Toll Free)
Fax: 816-968-2280
E-mail: sheedward@aol.com or natcath@aol.com
WWW homepage: natcath@aol.com
Marketing Director: Chuck Blakenship
Production Manager: Sarah Smiley
Publicity Coordinator: Sylvia Fox
Text Editor: Pat Marrin
Foreign Rights & Permis: Elyse Santome Chapela
Faith/denominational/cultural focus: Roman Catholic
Subject areas: Religious Life/Practice, Religious Thought/Theology, Religious Studies, Religion and Society, Sacred Literature, Religious Education
Types of publications: Electronic Publications, Reprints, Devotional Guides, Liturgical Materials, General Interest Nonfiction — Adult, General Interest Nonfiction — Juvenile, Self-Help, Dissertations
Sheed & Ward is committed to effective and responsible communication of the Roman Catholic vision of faith that does justice and peace. Our interest is primarily in theology, spirituality, pastoral ministry, and practical self-help. We believe that the clarity, strength and diversity of our Catholic tradition challenges the values and beliefs of our culture. We seek to encourage and enable authentic living of this tradition. To this end, we publish materials (books, videocassettes, pamphlets, programs) that deepen the understanding and practice of this faith that essentially includes an active option for justice at every level of private and public life.
Manuscript guidelines free upon request
Preferred form of initial contact: Short query or proposal package containing SASE, outline, and 3 sample chapters (or entire manuscript).
Send submissions to—
    Robert Heyer, Editor-in-Chief
Limitations/Restrictions: No simultaneous submissions accepted.

139   Signature Books
564 West 400 North, Salt Lake City, UT 84116-3411
Phone: 801-531-1483
Fax: 801-531-1488
E-mail: signature@thegulf.com
WWW homepage: signaturebooks.com
Publisher and President: George D. Smith
VP, Editor: Gary James Bergera
Publicist & Sec-Treas.: Ron Priddis
Production: Connie Disney
Business: Keiko Fukushima-Jones
Faith/denominational/cultural focus: Latter-Day Saint (Mormon)
Subject areas: Religious Biography, Doctrinal Theology & Dogma, History of Religion(s), Religion and Literature, Religion and Cultural/Ethnic Studies, Religion and Gender Studies, Book of Mormon — Commentary & Hermeneutics, Book of Mormon — Cultural & Historical Contexts
Types of publications: Electronic Publications (CD-ROM), Essay/Lecture Collections, Reprints, General Interest Nonfiction — Adult, Fiction — Adult, Poetry, Scholarly Monographs, General Reference
Our commitment is to enhancing scholarly and creative expression in the areas of Mormon studies—including history, theology, scripture, and culture—and western American history, biography, literature, and art. We also publish travel guides, humor, and books that deal with contemporary social issues—women's studies, gay and lesbian topics, ethnicity, the ACLU in Utah, etc.
Acquisitions focus for 1998-9: More of the same (western and Mormon Americana)
In print: 106 titles.   1997: 9 titles.
ISBN Prefix(es): 1-56085; 0-941214
Recent/Forthcoming Titles: *The Mormon Hierarchy: Extensions of Power*; *God the Mother and Other Theological Essays*; *Tabernacle Bar: A Novel*
Manuscript guidelines available only if proposal is accepted
Preferred form of initial contact: Short written query
Send submissions to—
    Gary James Bergera, Editor
Limitations/Restrictions: Authors must have publication record in professional journals.

140   Sixteenth Century Journal Pub, Inc
McClain Hill 111L, Truman State Univ., Kirksville, MO 63501-4221
Phone: 816-785-4665
Fax: 816-785-4181
President: R. V. Schnucker
Vice President: Robert McCune Kingdom
Secretary: Robert Kolb
Treasurer: Anna Mae Schnucker
Subject areas: Religion and Art, Religion and Literature, Early Modern
    History
Types of publications: Essay Collections, Scholarly Monographs
Acquisitions focus for 1998-9: We are looking for monographs in art
    history and literature for the early modern period.
In print: 30 titles.   1997: 6 titles.
ISBN Prefix(es): 0-940474
Recent/Forthcoming Titles: *Church Art and Architecture in the
    Netherlands Before 1556; Proceedings of the 4th International
    Calvin Congress; Civic Agendas and Religious Passion in 16th
    Century France*
No manuscript guidelines available
Preferred form of initial contact: Completed manuscript following
    Chicago Manual of Style 14th Ed. style
Send submissions to—
    Raymond Mentzer, Monograph Editor
Acquisitions address: History Department, Bozeman, MT 59717

141   Skinner House Books
Imprint of Unitarian Universalist Association
25 Beacon Street, Boston, MA 02108
Phone: 617-742-2100
Fax: 617-742-7025
E-mail: skinner_house@uua.org
WWW homepage: www.uua.org/skinner
Managing Editor: Patricia Frevert
Faith/denominational/cultural focus: Unitarian Universalist
Subject areas: Prayer & Meditation, Preaching & Homiletics, Spiritual
    Life/Personal Religion, Religious Biography, Doctrinal Theology &
    Dogma, Natural Theology, History of Religion(s)

Types of publications: Illustrated Books, Essay/Lecture Collections, Devotional Guides, Liturgical Materials, Translations

Skinner House Books aims to enrich the spiritual and religious lives of Unitarian Universalists and others who share the values of liberal religion. Skinner House publishes selected titles related to Unitarian Universalist faith, history, and beliefs—including historical documents central to the Unitarian and Universalist traditions.

Acquisitions focus for 1998-9: Books with wider appeal to all Unitarian Universalists and other religious liberals.

In print: 40 titles.   1997: 10 titles.

ISBN Prefix(es): 1-55896

Recent/Forthcoming Titles: *How to Preach a Sermon; For Faith and Freedom; Evening Tide*

Send #10 SASE for manuscript guidelines

Preferred form of initial contact: Proposal package containing SASE, outline, and 3 sample chapters.

Send submissions to—

Kristen Holmstrand, Assistant Editor

It is important for prospective authors to say in cover letter why Skinner House is the right publisher and to make a connection with Unitarian Universalism.

142   Snow Lion Publications, Inc

605 West State Street, PO Box 6483, Ithaca, NY 14851

Phone: 607-273-8519, 800-950-0313 (orders)

Fax: 607-273-8508

E-mail: tibet@snowlionpub.com

WWW homepage: www.snowlionpub.com

Faith/denominational/cultural focus: Tibetan Buddhism

Subject areas: Liturgy and Ritual, Prayer & Meditation, Spiritual Life/Personal Religion, Religion and Health, Religious Biography, Ethics, Doctrinal Theology & Dogma, History of Religion(s), Mythology, Folklore, Sacred Languages, Philosophy of Religion, Religion and Art, Religion and Literature, Religion and Classics, Religion and Gender Studies, Psychology of Religion, Sociology of Religion, Anthropology of Religion, Buddhist Literature — Commentary & Hermeneutics, Buddhist Literature — Translations, Religious Education — Seminary, Religious Education — Adult

Types of publications: Audio-Visual, Illustrated Books, Essay/Lecture
Collections, Reprints, Devotional Guides, Liturgical Materials,
General Interest Nonfiction — Adult, Self-Help, Fiction — Juvenile,
Dissertations, General Reference, Language Reference, Academic
Reference

Snow Lion Publications has developed a major library of Tibetan
Buddhism and culture with over 100 titles in print by most of the
major authors in the field. Snow Lion plans to fill out in English, the
key texts from the complete spectrum of religious and philosophic
traditions of Tibet.

In print: 110 titles.   1997: 15 titles.

ISBN Prefix(es): 0-937938, 1-55939

Recent/Forthcoming Titles: *Enthronement: The Recognition of the
Reincarnate Masters of Tibet and the Himalayas; Readings on the
Six Yogas of Naropa; Buddhist Advice for Living and Liberation:
Nagarjuna's Precious Garland*

Manuscript guidelines free upon request

Preferred form of initial contact: Proposal package containing outline
and 2-3 sample chapters.

Send submissions to—
    Sidney Piburn

143   Southeast Asia Publications, Northern Illinois University
Center for Southeast Asian Studies, Northern Illinois University,
    DeKalb, IL 60115
Phone: 815-753-1981
Fax: 815-753-1651
E-mail: seap@niu.edu
WWW homepage: www.niu.edu/acad/cseas/seap.html
Faith/denominational/cultural focus: Southeast Asia
Subject areas: Religious Life/Practice, Religious Thought/Theology,
Religious Studies, Religion and Society, Sacred Literature, Religious
Education
Types of publications: Classroom Instructional Materials,
Essay/Lecture Collections, General Interest Nonfiction — Adult,
Translations, Scholarly Monographs, General Reference, Language
Reference, Academic Reference
We publish scholarly books and articles on all aspects of Southeast
Asian studies, including religion.

In print: 10 titles.   1997: 1 title.   ISBN Prefix(es): 1-877979

Recent/Forthcoming Titles: Hunsaker, et al., *Loggers, Monks, Students, and Entrepreneurs: Four Essays on Thailand*; Rhum, *The Ancestral Lords: Gender, Descent, and Spirits in a Northern Thai Village*; Durrenberger, *Lisu Religion*

Manuscript guidelines free upon request

Preferred form of initial contact: Short written query or proposal package containing SASE, outline and sample chapters.

Send submissions to—
   Edwin Zehner, Director

144   Standard Publishing

Subsidiary/division of Standex International Corporation

8121 Hamilton Ave, Cincinnati, OH 45231

Phone: 800-543-1301

Fax: 513-931-0950

Director, Curriculum: Dick McKinley

Director, VBS: Phyllis Sanders

Director, New Products: Diane Stortz

Faith/denominational/cultural focus: Interdenominational Christian (Bible-based)

Subject areas: Religious Education — Preschool, Elementary, and Adult.

Types of publications: Classroom Instructional Texts, Illustrated Books

Standard Publishing publishes Christian education resources and curriculum for church and home.

Acquisitions focus for 1998-9: Administrative helps for ministry leaders.

Recent/Forthcoming Titles: *Child-Sensitive Teaching*; *Baby's First Bible*; *Kids Can Explore the Bible*

Send #10 SASE for manuscript guidelines

Preferred form of initial contact: Proposal package containing SASE, outline, 2-3 sample chapters, and author biography as needed.

Send submissions to—
   Christian education: Ruth Frederick
   Children's books: Greg Holder
   Drama resources: Lise Caldwell
   Youth resources: Dale Reeves

Limitations/Restrictions: When writing for children, establish yourself as a writer in magazine markets first.

Many of our projects are developed in house or on assignment

145 State University of New York Press

State University Plaza, Albany, NY 12246-0001
Book Orders: State University of New York Press, c/o CUP Services,
   PO Box 6525, Ithaca, NY 14851
Phone: 518-472-5000, 800-666-2211 (orders), 607-277-2211 (Cust. Svc.)
Fax: 518-472-5038
WWW homepage: www.sunypress.edu
Subject areas: Religious Studies, Religion and Society, Sacred
   Literature
Types of pubns: Essay/Lecture Collections, Scholarly Monographs
SUNY Press publishes a wide range of works in the academic study of
   religion. Our program includes both eastern and western religions,
   religion and society, and sociology of religion.
Manuscript guidelines free upon request
Preferred form of initial contact: Proposal package containing outline,
   2-3 sample chapters, author's estimation of work's market.
Send submissions to—
   Nancy Ellegate, Acquisitions Editor
Complete manuscripts are welcome; do not bind or staple materials.

146   Swedenborg Association

278-A Meeting Street, Charleston, SC 29401
Phone: 803-853-6211
Fax: 803-853-0920
E-mail: arcana@worldnet.att.net
WWW homepage: www.evpro.com/swedenborg
Faith/denominational/cultural focus: New Church; Esotersim
Subject areas: Spiritual Life/Personal Religion, Doctrinal Theology &
   Dogma, Systematic Theology, Comparative Religions, Religion and
   Literature, Sacred Literature — Commentary & Hermeneutics
   (Swedenborg)
Types of publications: Essay/Lecture Collections, Reprints, Scholarly
   Monographs
The Swedenborg Association specializes in publishing works by or about
   Emanuel Swedenborg, his influence, his teachings, and comparative
   studies of Swednborg and other religious traditions. The quarterly
   journal Arcana is dedicated to exploring spiritual topics in the light
   of Swedenborg's teachings and the teachings of the world's religious
   traditions, and to showing the fundamental agreement between
   religious traditions: the *religio perennis*.

Acquisitions focus for 1998-9: Swedenborg; Esoterism; New Church.
In print: 19 titles.   1997: 3 titles.
Manuscript guidelines free upon request
Preferred form of initial contact: Short written query
Send submissions to—
  Drake Kaiser

147   Swedenborg Foundation
320 N Church St, West Chester, PA 19380
Orders: SCB Distributors, 15608 S New Drive, Ardena, CA 90248
Phone: 610-430-3222, 800-719-6423 (orders)
Fax: 610-430-7982
E-mail: info@swedenborg.com
WWW homepage: www.swedenborg.com
Editor: Mary Lou Bertucci
Marketing: Susan Picard
Faith/denominational/cultural focus: Swedenborgian, Interfaith
Subject areas: Spiritual Life/Personal Religion, Religion and Health, Religious Biography, Religious Thought/Theology, Comparative Religions, Interdisciplinary Studies, Sacred Lit. — Translations
Types of publications: Essay/Lecture Collections, Reprints, General Interest Nonfiction — Adult, Translations, Self-Help, Scholarly Monographs, Dissertations
We publish books by and about Emanuel Swedenborg, 18th Century scientist and spiritual visionary: monographs and trade books (Chrysalis Books) dealing with Swedenborgian thought and theology and/or related topics (e.g. Biblical interpretation, spiritual growth, angels and spirits, near death, death and dying, the afterlife, application of spiritual principles to daily living).
Acquisitions focus for 1998-9: Recovery/spirituality, psychology of religion, religious symbolism, practical spirituality, spirituality in a material population. Especially sought are nonfiction works that bridge contemporary issues to spiritual insights.
In print: 75 titles.   1997: 5 titles.   ISBN Prefix(es): 0-87785
Recent/Forthcoming Titles: *Psychology of Spiritual Healing; Tunnel to Eternity; Return to the Promised Land*
Manuscript guidelines free upon request
Preferred form of initial contact: Short written query (1 page)
Send submissions to—
  Susan Poole, Acquisitions Editor

148   Templeton Foundation Press
Two Radnor Corporate Center, Suite 320, 100 Matsonford Rd,
   Radnor, PA 19087
Phone: 610-687-8942
Fax: 610-687-8961
E-mail: tfp@templeton.org
WWW homepage: www.templeton.org
Dir. of Publications: Joanna V. Hill
Subject areas: Spiritual Life/Personal Religion, Religion and the
   Family, Religion and Health, Religious Biography, Ethics in relation
   to moral education, Religion and the Physical Sciences, Religion in
   Popular Culture/Media, Religious Education — Secondary,
   Religious Education — Post-Secondary
Types of publications: Books-on-Tape, Audio-Visual, Illustrated Books,
   Essay/Lecture Collections, General Interest Nonfiction — Adult,
   Self-Help, Scholarly Monographs, Academic Reference
Templeton Foundation Press publishes non-fiction books in the
   following areas: the relationship between science and religion; the
   relationship between spirituality and health; moral education; free
   enterprise education; and the scientific verification of basic spiritual
   principles.
In print: 1 title.   1997: 5 titles.
ISBN Prefix(es): 1-890151
Recent/Forthcoming Titles: *Worldwide Laws of Life: 200 Eternal
   Spiritual Principles*; *Golden Nuggets*; *How Large is God?: The
   Voices of Scientists and Theologians*
Manuscript guidelines free upon request
Preferred form of initial contact: Proposal package containing SASE,
   outline and 1 sample chapter.
Send submissions to—
   Joanna V. Hill, Dir. of Publications

149   Temple University Press
USB 305, 1601 N Broad St, Philadelphia, PA 19122
Phone: 215-204-8787
Fax: 215-204-4719
E-mail: tempress@astro.ocis.temple.edu
WWW homepage: www.temple.edu/tempress

Subject areas: Sociology of Religion, Anthropology of Religion, Religion and Society

Types of publications: General Interest Nonfiction — Adult, Scholarly Monographs

Temple University Press publishes elected titles in religion and society focusing on human rights, sociology and anthropology of religion.

No manuscript guidelines available

Preferred form of initial contact: Short written query

Send submissions to—

Doris B. Braendel, Senior Acquisitions Editor

150   Treehaus Communications

906 W Loveland Ave, PO Box 249, Loveland, OH 45140-0249

Phone: 513-683-5716

Fax: 513-683-2882

E-mail: gaphaus@aol.com

Faith/denominational/cultural focus: Roman Catholic, Episcopal, Lutheran

Subject areas: Liturgy and Ritual, Spiritual Life/Personal Religion, Religion and the Family, Spiritual Life of Children, Religious Education — Theory and Methodology, Religious Education — Elementary, Religious Education — Secondary

Types of publications: Classroom Instructional Materials, Audio-Visual, Liturgical Materials (especially for children)

We publish print and electronic media materials related to nurturing the spiritual life of children, particularly through ritual and story. Our publications for children and adults aim to develop the skills necessary to living reflective lives.

Acquisitions focus for 1998-9: We seek work for children and/or adults that respects the innate spirituality of children.

In print: 40+ titles.   1997: 7 titles.

Recent/Forthcoming Titles: Jeannine Schmid, Ph.D., *Nurturing Your Child's Spirit: A Montessorian Approach*; Gianna Gobbi, *Feed My Lambs: The Montessori Principles Applied to the Catechesis of Children*; Pottebaum and Wickel, *Bread of Life: A Family Spiritual Life Journal*

No manuscript guidelines available

Preferred form of initial contact: Proposal package containing outline and 1 or 2 sample chapters.

Send submissions to—Gerard A. Pottebaum, Publisher

151   Trinity Press International
Subsidiary/division of The Morehouse Group
PO Box 1321, Harrisburg, PA 17105
Phone: 717-541-8130, 800-877-0012 (orders)
Fax: 717-541-8136, 717-541-8128 (orders)
Publisher: Harold W. Rast
Managing Editor: Laura Barrett
Faith/denominational/cultural focus: Interfaith
Subject areas: Liturgy and Ritual, Preaching & Homiletics, Missions,
   Ethics, Doctrinal Theology & Dogma, Process Theology, Systematic
   Theology, Pastoral Theology, Natural Theology, Theological
   Education (Methodology), Religion and Classics, Religion and
   Cultural/Ethnic Studies, Religion and Gender Studies, Religion and
   Archaeology, Religion in Popular Culture/Media, Religion and
   Public Policy, Sacred Literature — Commentary & Hermeneutics,
   Sacred Literature — Cultural & Historical Contexts, Sacred
   Literature — Translations, Religious Education — Theory and
   Methodology, Religious Education — Seminary, Religious
   Education — Adult
Types of publications: Liturgical Materials, Translations, Scholarly
   Monographs, Academic Reference
Trinity Press International is an independent, ecumenical, and
   interreligious publisher whose goal is to create a strong and
   vigorous literature that will enlighten and quicken religious thought
   and action throughout the world. The Press therefore provides
   serious and accessible books, often interdisciplinary in character, for
   a broad range of readers that address the deepest questions human
   beings ask, and that assist in the formation of intelligent, moral, and
   effective faith communities of the future.
Acquisitions focus for 1998-9: Biblical studies, theological studies,
   African-American religious thought and life, religion and society,
   and Anglican issues.
In print: 248 titles.   1997: 35 titles.
ISBN Prefix(es): 1-56338, 0-334
Recent/Forthcoming Titles: Birger Pearson, *The Emergence of the
   Christian Religion: Essays on Early Christianity*; H. Edward
   Everding, et al, *Viewpoints: Perspectives of Faith and Christian
   Nurture*; Jack Kingsbury, *Gospel Interpretation: Narrative-Critical
   and Social Scientific Approaches*
Manuscript guidelines free upon request.

Preferred form of initial contact: Proposal package containing short cover letter, SASE, outline, and 2 sample chapters.
Send submissions to—
    Harold W. Rast, Th.D., Publisher

152   Tyndale House Publishers
351 Executive Dr, PO Box 80, Wheaton, IL 60189
Phone: 630-668-8300
Fax: 630-668-8311
WWW homepage: www.tyndale.com
CEO & President: Mark Taylor
CFO: Paul Matthews
Corporate VP: Doug Knox
Owner/Chmn of the Board: Ken Taylor
Faith/denominational/cultural focus: Evangelical Christian
Subject areas: Prayer & Meditation, Spiritual Life/Personal Religion, Religion and the Family, Doctrinal Theology & Dogma, Psychology of Religion, Religion in Popular Culture/Media, Biblical Literature — Commentary & Hermeneutics, Biblical Literature — Translations
Types of publications: Books-on-Tape, Electronic Publications, Illustrated Books, Reprints, Devotional Guides, General Interest Nonfiction — Adult, Fiction — Adult, Translations, Self-Help, Fiction — Juvenile, General Reference
Our corporate purpose is to minister to the spiritual needs of people, primarily through literature consistent with Biblical principles. Our list includes nonfiction, fiction, Bibles, audio products, videos, foreign books, calendars, and computer software.
Acquisitions focus for 1998-9: Launching romance fiction line, strengthening Christian living line, and expanding fiction; find fresh approach to devotional materials.
In print: 1000 titles.   1997: 100 titles.
ISBN Prefix(es): 0-8423
Recent/Forthcoming Titles: James Dobson, *Solid Answers*; Charles Colson, *Burden of Truth*; *The Focus on the Family Complete Book of Baby and Child Care*
Send SASE for manuscript guidelines
Preferred form of initial contact: Agented submissions only (we only accept submissions through Karen Voke)

153 United Church Press
Subsidiary/division of United Church Board for Homeland Ministries
700 Prospect Ave E, Cleveland, OH 44114-1100
Phone: 216-736-3715, 800-654-5129 (orders)
Fax: 216-736-3703, 216-736-3713 (orders)
E-mail: ucpress@ucc.org
Publisher: Lynne Deming, Ph.D.
Faith/denominational/cultural focus: Ecumenical, United Church of Christ
Subject areas: Prayer & Meditation, Vocational/Pastoral Guidance, Preaching & Homiletics, Religion and the Family, Pastoral Theology, Religion and Cultural/Ethnic Studies, Religion and Gender Studies, Religious Education — Elementary, Religious Education — Secondary, Religious Education — Post-Secondary, Religious Education — Adult
Types of publications: Classroom Instructional Materials, Music, Devotional Guides, Liturgical Materials, Self-Help, Gen'l Reference
United Church Press focuses on church life and ministry with specialties in multicultural and liberation themes.
In print: 100 titles.   1997: 20 titles.
ISBN Prefix(es): 0-8298
Recent/Forthcoming Titles: *Navigating the Deep River: Spirituality in African American Families*; *The Book of Daily Prayer*; *Feasting with God: Adventures in Table Spirituality*
Manuscript guidelines free upon request
Preferred form of initial contact: Proposal package containing short written query, SASE, 1 sample chapter, and author's résumé.
Send submissions to—
    Kim Sadler, Editor
Limitations/Restrictions: No materials returned without SASE.

154   University of Chicago Press
5801 S Ellis Ave, Chicago, IL 60637
Orders: 11030 S Langley Ave, Chicago, IL 60628
Phone: 773-702-7700, 800-621-2736 (orders),
    773-568-1550 (international orders)
Fax: 773-702-9756, 800-621-8476 (orders)
WWW homepage: www.press.uchicago.edu
Subject areas: Ethics, Comparative Religions, History of Religion(s), Mythology, Philosophy of Religion, Religion and Art, Religion and Literature, Religion and Classics, Religion and Cultural/Ethnic Studies, Religion and Gender Studies, Sociology of Religion, Anthropology of Religion, Religion and Political Science, Religion and the Natural Sciences, Religion in Popular Culture/Media, Religion and Law, Religion and Public Policy, Talmudic Literature — Translations, Sacred Literature — Cultural & Historical Contexts, Buddhist Literature — Translations, Taoist Literature — Translations, Religious Education — Theory and Methodology
Types of publications: Illustrated Books, Reprints, Translations, Scholarly Monographs, General Reference, Language Reference, Academic Reference
Acquisitions focus for 1998-9: Titles for the "Religion and Postmodernism" and "Chicago Studies in the History of Judaism" series; also studies of American religions and popular culture.
1997: 30 titles.
ISBN Prefix(es): 0-226
Recent/Forthcoming Titles: Regina H. Schwartz, *The Curse of Cain: The Violent Legacy of Monotheism*; James Gilbert, *Redeeming Culture: American Religion in an Age of Science, 1925-1962*; A. Eisen, *Rethinking Modern Judaism: Ritual, Commandment, Community*
No manuscript guidelines available
Preferred form of initial contact: Proposal package containing SASE, outline, and one sample chapter.
Send submissions to—
    Religious studies: Alan G. Thomas, Senior Editor
    Philosophy and anthropology: T. David Brent, Senior Editor
    Sociology: Douglas Mitchell, Senior Editor
    Law: John Tryneski, Senior Editor
    Reference: Penelope Kaiserlian, Associate Director
Limitations/Restrictions: No telephone or e-mail inquiries, please.

155   University of Illinois Press
1325 S Oak St, Champaign, IL 61820
Orders/Warehouse: PO Box 4856, Hampden PO, Baltimore, MD 21211
Phone: 217-333-0950, 800-545-4703 (orders—U.S.),
    410-516-6927 (orders—MD, USA & Canada)
Fax: 217-244-8082, 410-516-6969 (orders)
E-mail: uipress@uiuc.edu
WWW homepage: www.uiuc.edu/providers/uipress
Director: Richard L. Wentworth
Dir. of Marketing: David M. Perkins
Sales Manager: Katherine Dressel
Production Manager: Mary Lou Menches
Art Director: Copenhaver Cumpston
Business Manager: William C. Ackermann
Journals Manager: Ann Lowry
Development Director: Judith M. McCulloh
Associate Director: Elizabeth G. Dulaney
Managing Editor: Theresa L. Sears
Subject areas: Religion and Society
Types of publications: Essay Collections, Scholarly Monographs
University of Illinois Press has a strong focus on U.S. social history, so
    we welcome manuscripts that fall in that category: in general, works
    that explore any aspect of religion and/in society are appropriate. In
    addition, we have a series, Studies in Anglican History (edited by
    Peter W. Williams at Miami University), and a long-standing list in
    Mormon studies. As a university press all our titles undergo a
    rigorous peer review and revision process before acceptance.
In print: 130 titles.   1997: 10 titles.
ISBN Prefix(es): 0-252
Recent/Forthcoming Titles: Jonathan Sarna (ed.), *Minority Faiths and
    the American Protestant Mainstream*; John K. Roth, *Private Needs,
    Public Selves: Talk about Religion in America*; Peter W. Williams,
    Houses of God: Region, Religion, and Architecture in the U.S.
Manuscript guidelines free upon request
Preferred form of initial contact: Proposal package containing short
    query, SASE, outline, and 1 or 2 sample chapters.
Send submissions to—
    Elizabeth G. Dulany, Associate Director

156 University of Notre Dame Press

PO Box L, Notre Dame, IN 46556

Orders: University of Notre Dame Press, Chicago Distribution Center, 11030 S Langley Ave, Chicago, IL 60628

Phone: 219-631-6346, 800-621-2736 (orders)

Fax: 219-631-8148, 800-621-8476 (orders)

E-mail: undpress.1@nd.edu

Subject areas: Liturgy and Ritual, Prayer & Meditation, Spiritual Life/Personal Religion, Religion and Health, Religious Biography, Ethics, Systematic Theology, Pluralistic/Ecumenical Theology, History of Religion(s), Philosophy of Religion, Religion and Art, Religion and Literature, Religion and Cultural/Ethnic Studies, Psychology of Religion, Sociology of Religion, Anthropology of Religion, Religion and the Physical Sciences, Religion and the Natural Sciences, Religion and Law, Religion and Public Policy, Sacred Literature — Cultural & Historical Contexts, Religious Education — Post-Secondary

Types of publications: Books-on-Tape, Reprints, General Interest Nonfiction — Adult, Translations, Scholarly Monographs, General Reference

Our mission includes the goal of publishing the very best authors writing in theology, ethics, philosophy of religion, religious history, and other subject areas mentioned above. We also publish books which highlight the lives, work, and ministries of committed individuals, both historical and contemporary, who make a difference for good in the world.

Acquisitions focus for 1998-9: Biography, ethics, social justice ministries, philosophy of religion, and psychology of religion.

In print: 500 titles.   1997: 30 titles.

ISBN Prefix(es): 0268-

Recent/Forthcoming Titles: *Born of Common Hungers*; *Sacred Passion: The Art of William Schickel*; Fergus Kerr, *Immortal Longings*

No manuscript guidelines available

Preferred form of initial contact: Short written query or proposal package containing outline, sample chapter, table of contents, expected length of manuscript.

Send submissions to—

Biography, social justice ministry: Jeffrey Gaineig, Assoc. Director

Ethics/philosophy of religion: James Langford, Executive Director

Limitations/Restrictions: Please do not send full manuscript without invitation; sample material cannot be returned without SASE.

157   University of Scranton Press
Subsidiary/division of University of Scranton
Linden & Monroe, Scranton, PA 18510
Phone: 717-941-4228
Fax: 717-941-4309
WWW homepage: www.academic.uofs.edu/organization/upress
Director: Richard W. Rousseau
Faith/denominational/cultural focus: Roman Catholic
Subject areas: Religious Thought/Theology, Comparative Religions, Philosophy of Religion, Religion and Art, Religion and Literature, Psychology of Religion, Religion and Society, Biblical Literature — Commentary & Hermeneutics, Biblical Literature — Philology & Linguistics, Biblical Literature — Translations, Religious Education — Seminary, Religious Education — Adult
Types of publications: Illustrated Books, Essay/Lecture Collections, Reprints, Translations, Scholarly Monographs, General Reference
The cutting edge of various theological disciplines examined in the Catholic tradition; philosophy of religion and the culture of northeastern Pennsylvania.
In print: 31 title. 1997: 5 titles.
ISBN Prefix(es): 0-940866
Recent/Forthcoming Titles: *Religious Values of the Terminally Ill: Handbook for Health Professionals*; *The Spiritual Legacy of Friedrich von Hugel*; *From Then Until Now: William Kennedy's Albany Novels*
Manuscript guidelines free upon request
Preferred form of initial contact: Short written query
Send submissions to—
    Richard W. Rousseau, Director
Limitations/Restrictions: No poetry or fiction.

158   University of South Carolina Press
937 Assembly St, 8th Floor, Columbia, SC 29203
Orders, Business Office: 718 Devine St, Columbia, SC 29208
Phone: 803-777-5243
Fax: 803-777-0160
E-mail: thdavis@gwm.sc.edu
WWW homepage: gopher.press.sc.edu

Subject areas: Religious Biography, Biblical Literature — Commentary & Hermeneutics, Biblical Lit. — Cultural & Historical Contexts

Types of publications: Scholarly Monographs, Academic Reference

The Press publishes three series—Studies in Comparative Religion (ed. Frederick M. Denny); Studies on Personalities of the Old Testament (ed. James L. Crenshaw); and Studies on Personalities of the New Testament (ed. D. Moody Smith)—as well as individual titles in American religion, especially the American South and the black church.

In print: 34 titles.   1997: 5 titles.

ISBN Prefix(es): 1-57003

Recent/Forthcoming Titles: Fatemeh Keshavarz, *Reading Mystical Lyric: The Case of Jalal al-Din Rumi*; John Painter, *Just James: The Brother of Jesus in History and Tradition*; Janet Cornelius, *The Religious Mission to the Slave*

Manuscript guidelines free upon request

Preferred form of initial contact: Proposal package containing SASE, outline, 1-2 sample chapters, and author's C.V.

Send submissions to—
     Barry Blose, Acquisitions Editor

159   University of Tennessee Press

293 Communications Building, University of Tennessee,
     Knoxville, TN 37996-0325

Orders: Chicago Distribution Center, 11030 S Langley Ave,
     Chicago, IL 60628

Phone: 423-974-3321, 800-621-2736 (orders)

Fax: 423-974-3724, 773-660-2235 (orders)

E-mail: harrisj@utk.edu

WWW homepage: www.lib.utk.edu/UTKgophers/UT-PRESS

Subject areas: Religious Biography, History of Religion(s), Folklore, Religion and Cultural/Ethnic Studies, Sociology of Religion, Religion in Popular Culture/Media

Types of publications: Scholarly Monographs

The University of Tennessee Press' religion list concentrates on religion in the United States. We are particularly strong in, and encourage submissions in, African-American religion, religion in Appalachia, and religion in the South.

Acquisitions focus for 1998-9: Our publishing program in religious studies will continue to grow, but we will not be adding new areas of concentration.

In print: 45 titles.   1997: 5 titles.

ISBN Prefix(es): 0-87049

Recent/Forthcoming Titles: William J. Weston, *Presbyterian Pluralism: Competition in a Protestant House*; David L. Kimbrough, *Reverend Joseph Tarkington, Methodist Circuit Rider: From Frontier Evangelism to Refined Religion*; Howard Dorgan, *In the Hands of a Happy God: The "No-Hellers" of Central Appalachia*

Manuscript guidelines free upon request

Preferred form of initial contact: Proposal package containing short query, SASE, outline, 3-5 sample chapters, and current C.V. Telephone and e-mail inquiries accepted.

Send submissions to—

Joyce Harrison, Acquisitions Editor

160   University Press of America

4720 Boston Way, Lanham, MD 20706

Phone: 301-459-3366, 800-462-6420 (ordering/customer service)

Fax: 301-459-2118

E-mail: njulrich@univpress.com

WWW homepage: www.univpress.com

Publisher: James E. Lyons

Editor-in-Chief: Jonathan Sisk

Subject areas: Religious Thought/Theology, Religious Studies, Religion and Society, Sacred Literature, Religious Education

Types of publications: Classroom Instructional Materials, Essay/Lecture Collections, Reprints, Translations, Scholarly Monographs, Dissertations, General Reference, Language Reference, Academic Reference

For over twenty years, UPA has been a leading publisher in religious studies. Proudly serving the academic community, we specialize in Judaic studies, theology, and the history of religion. However, we welcome the opportunity to review scholarly manuscripts in all areas of religious studies.

In print: 300+ titles.   1997: 70 titles.

ISBN Prefix(es): 0-7618, 0-8191

Recent/Forthcoming Titles: *Major Modern and Contemporary Theologies; Introduction to the Bible, vol. 1; East Wind: Taoist and Cosmological Implications of Christian Theology*
Manuscript guidelines free upon request
Preferred form of initial contact: Proposal package containing SASE, outline, 2 sample chapters, author's resume or C.V.
Send submissions to—
Acquisitions Editor, Nancy Ulrich

161   University Press of Virginia
3608 University Station, Charlottesville, VA 22903
Phone: 804-924-3468, 804-982-3033 (editorial), 804-924-3469 (orders)
Fax: 804-982-2655
WWW homepage: www.upress.virginia.edu
Subject areas: Ethics, Comparative Religions, History of Religion(s), Mythology, Folklore, Philosophy of Religion, Religion and Art, Religion and Music, Religion and Literature, Religion and Cultural/Ethnic Studies, Religion and Gender Studies, Psychology of Religion, Sociology of Religion, Anthropology of Religion, Methodologies of Study and Teaching, Religion and Society
Types of publications: Classroom Instructional Materials, Essay/Lecture Collections, Reprints, Translations, Scholarly Monographs
Our series of studies in religion and culture focuses on questions of interpretation of religious and cultural traditions and the interplay between them. The series includes interdisciplinary and cross-cultural approaches. What unifies the series is a set of shared issues and questions rather than a single religious tradition, academic discipline, or cultural focus. These shared concerns have to do with the meanings of religious and cultural traditions in view of the challenges presented by the late Twentieth Century.
Acquisitions focus for 1998-9: Studies in religion and culture—may be cross-cultural and/or interdisciplinary; contemporary focus.
In print: 13 titles.
ISBN Prefix(es): 0-8139
Recent/Forthcoming Titles: Laurie L. Patton and Wendy Doniger, ed., *Myth and Method*; David Chidester, *Savage Systems: Colonialism and Comparative Religion in Southern Africa*; Gary L. Ebersole,

Captured by Texts: Puritan to Postmodern Images of Indian Captivity
Manuscript guidelines free upon request
Preferred form of initial contact: Proposal package containing cover letter presenting the project, outline, and authors C.V.
Send submissions to—
Cathie Brettschneider, Humanities Editor
Limitations/Restrictions: Do not send whole (or even partial) manuscripts without invitation.
Double-space all submitted material; use endnotes instead of footnotes; have text on 1 side of page only; do not use proportional font or other design features (italic/bold type).

162   Upper Room Books

Subsidiary/division of The Upper Room
1908 Grand Ave, PO Box 189, Nashville, TN 37212
Phone: 615-340-7000, 800-972-0433 (orders)
Fax: 615-640-7006
WWW homepage: www.upperroom.org
World Editor: Stephen Bryant
Dir. Int'l Rights & Permissions: Sarah Schaller-Linn
Faith/denominational/cultural focus: Interdenominational Christian
Subject areas: Prayer & Meditation, Vocational/Pastoral Guidance, Spiritual Life/Personal Religion, Religion and the Family, Religion and Health, Religious Education — Elementary, Religious Education — Secondary, Religious Education — Adult
Types of publications: Reprints, Devotional Guides, General Interest Nonfiction — Adult, Self-Help
Upper Room Books publishes resources that offer individuals and groups the promise of a life-giving relationship with God and assist them in their continuing journey toward spiritual maturity by providing guidance for a disciplined life of prayer and active Christian response. In content, focus, language, art, and illustrations, Upper Room Books seeks to publish resources that reflect the ethnic, cultural, and age diversity of the global Christian community.
Acquisitions focus for 1998-9: For clergy and congregational leaders: shaping and transforming communities, nurturing their own spiritual journey, and assisting people in the practice of spiritual

disciplines. For laity: understanding the spiritual life and recognizing gifts and challenges. For families: nurturing family spiritual life.
In print: 215 titles.   1997: 28 titles.
ISBN Prefix(es): 0-8358
Recent/Forthcoming Titles: Betty Cloyd, *Children and Prayer*; Joyce Hollyday, *Then Shall Your Light Rise: Spiritual Formation and Social Witness*; David M. Griebner, *The Carpenter and the Unbuilder: Stories for the Spiritual Quest*
Send #10 SASE for manuscript guidelines.
Preferred form of initial contact: Proposal package containing SASE, outline, and 2-3 sample chapters.
Limitations/Restrictions: No poetry or fiction.

163   U.S. Publishers
PO Box 1171, Pebble Beach, CA 93953
Phone: 408-372-5590
Fax: 408-375-4525
Subject areas: Critique of Religion
Types of publications: Self-Help
It is our belief that the frail human episode has abused a given relationship with God the Creator, both male and female. All organized religions developed by western and eastern civilizations have selected self-serving aspects from ancient religious teaching, such as found in the Egyptian system of spiritual cultivation and the Kamitic initiation system to conquer evil existing on Earth. In so doing they have become part of that evil and dwell obviously in opposition to God.
Acquisitions focus for 1998-9: Open-minded about subject; we want nothing from fools called scholars who continue the depraved status of humanity in accepted dogma.
Recent/Forthcoming Titles: A. K. Karsky, *The Case Against Religion*
Preferred form of initial contact:
Limitations/Restrictions: Nothing about organized religion will be considered.
Write for our market: "believers" who question their beliefs.

164   Vedanta Press
Subsidiary/division of Vedanta Society of Southern California
1946 Vedanta Place, Los Angeles, CA 90068
Phone: 213-960-1727
Fax: 213-465-9568
E-mail: bob@vedanta.org
WWW homepage: www.vedanta.com/www.vedanta.org
Manager: Robert Adjemian
Faith/denominational/cultural focus: Vedanta
Subject areas: Prayer & Meditation, Spiritual Life/Personal Religion,
    Religious Biography, Comparative Religions, Mythology,
    Philosophy of Religion, Psychology of Religion, Vedanta/Hindu
    Sacred Literature
Types of publications: Essay/Lecture Collections, General Interest
    Nonfiction — Adult, Translations, Self-Help
Vedanta Press publishes books on the philosophy, teachings, and
    personalities of the Vedanta movement.
No manuscript guidelines available
No unsolicited submissions accepted (Thus far, we only publish within
    our organization).

165   Veritas Press
PO Box 1704, Santa Monica, CA 90406
Phone: 310-393-7700
Director: J. Peters
Faith/denominational/cultural focus: Roman Catholic
Subject areas: Liturgy and Ritual, Doctrinal Theology & Dogma,
    Religion in Popular Culture/Media
Types of publications: Liturgical Materials, Scholarly Monographs
Veritas Press specializes in publishing traditional Catholic liturgical
    (Tridentine) materials and scholarly books regarding the Church in
    the modern world.
Acquisitions focus for 1998-9: Moral theology.
In print: 25 titles.
Recent/Forthcoming Titles: Hertz, *On the Contrary*; *Revised New
    Marian Missal*; *Handbook of Moral Theology for High School and
    College Students*

No manuscript guidelines available
Preferred form of initial contact: Short written query
Limitations/Restrictions: We do not have the resources to publish new
   authors at this time.

166   Virgil Hensely Publishing
6116 E 32nd St, Tulsa, OK 74135
Phone: 918-664-8520
Fax: 918-664-8562
Faith/denominational/cultural focus: Christian
Subject areas: Prayer & Meditation, Vocational/Pastoral Guidance,
   Spiritual Life/Personal Religion, Religion and the Family, Doctrinal
   Theology & Dogma, Religion and Gender Studies, Religious
   Education — Elementary, Religious Education — Secondary,
   Religious Education — Adult
Types of publications: Classroom Instructional Materials, General
   Interest Nonfiction — Adult, General Interest Nonfiction —
   Juvenile, Translations, Self-Help, General Reference, Church
   Stewardship Programs
We publish books, Bible studies and direct-mail stewardship program.
   We are a non-denominational publisher. We look for works that
   cross denominational lines and are directed toward the large
   Christian market, not small, specialized groups. No new age.
1997: 4 titles.
ISBN Prefix(es): 1-56322
Recent/Forthcoming Titles: *How to Reach Your Church's Financial
   Goals This Year, 30th ed.; Couples in the Bible: Examples to Live By;
   When All You Can Do Is Wait*
Send #10 SASE for manuscript guidelines
Preferred form of initial contact: Proposal package containing cover
   letter, SASE, and 1st 3 chapters.
Send submissions to—
   Terri Kalfas, Editor

167   Volcano Press, Inc
PO Box 270, Volcano, CA 95689-0270
E-mail orders: sales@volcanopress.com
Phone: 209-296-3445, 800-879-9636 (orders)
Fax: 209-296-4515
E-mail: ruth@volcanopress.com
WWW homepage: www.volcanopress.com
Subject areas: Vocational/Pastoral Guidance, Religion and the Family, Religion and Law
Types of publications: Essay/Lecture Collections, Reprints, Self-Help
Volcano Press publishes the 'Family Violence and Religion: An Interfaith Resource Guide,' a compendium containing articles and excerpts designed to assist clergy and church workers of all faiths to counsel abused women and abusive men to understand the myths and facts about domestic violence, and to provide sermon development ideas.
Acquisitions focus for 1998-9: Family violence issues.
In print: 1 title.
ISBN Prefix(es): 1-884244
Recent/Forthcoming Titles: *Learning to Live Without Violence: A Handbook for Men* (available in Spanish under the title *Apvender a Vivir Sin Violencia*)
No manuscript guidelines available
Preferred form of initial contact: Short written query & SASE.
Send submissions to—
    Ruth Gottstein

168   Wadsworth Publishing
Subsidiary/division of ITP
10 Davis Drive, Belmont, CA 94002
Phone: 415-595-2350
Fax: 415-637-7544
E-mail: padams@wadsworth.com
WWW homepage: www.thomson.com/wadsworth.html
Subject areas: Spiritual Life/Personal Religion, Religious Biography, Ethics, Comparative Religions, History of Religion(s), Philosophy of Religion, Religion and Gender Studies, Sociology of Religion, Religion in Popular Culture/Media, Sacred Literature — Cultural & Historical Contexts

Types of publications: Classroom Instructional Materials, Audio-Visual, Electronic Publications

Wadsworth is a higher education publisher which focuses on textbooks for commonly offered undergraduate courses at all colleges and universities.

Acquisitions focus for 1998-9: Introduction to religion, comparative religions, ethics, and multi-media.

In print: 37 titles.   1997: 3 titles.

ISBN Prefix(es): 0-534

Recent/Forthcoming Titles: Weaver, Brakke, and Bivins, *Introduction to Christianity, 3rd ed.*; Paper and Thompson, *The Chinese Way in Religion, 2nd ed.*; Neusner, *The Way of the Torah, 6th ed.*

Manuscript guidelines free upon request

Preferred form of initial contact: Short written query (by e-mail).

Send submissions to—

   Peter Adams, Editor

169   Samuel Weiser Inc

PO Box 612, York Beach, ME 03910

Phone: 207-363-4393

Fax: 207-363-5799

E-mail: weiserbooks@worldnet.att.net

Publisher: Donald Weiser

Vice President: Betty Lundsted

Faith/denominational/cultural focus: Eastern Philosophy, Mysticism, Kabbalah

Subject areas: Liturgy and Ritual, Prayer & Meditation, Spiritual Life/Personal Religion, Mythology, Folklore, Psychology of Religion, Sacred Literature — Translations

Types of publications: Reprints, General Interest Nonfiction — Adult, Translations, Self-Help, General Reference

We publish books relating to Eastern philosophy and all facets of the secret and hidden teaching of the mystical tradition stemming from Judeo-Christian beliefs. We publish books that are the lifework of the author. We want books written by teachers or by people who have studied extensively. We don't want library researched rehashes of what has gone before. We are a backlist publisher.

In print: 150 titles.   1997: 10 titles.

ISBN Prefix(es): 0-87728, 1-57863

Recent/Forthcoming Titles: Rabbi Aryeh Kaplan, *Sefer Yetzirah*; T. Schipflinger, *Sophia Maria: A Holistic Vision of Creation*; Master Nan Huai Chin, *Basic Buddhism: Exploring Buddhism and Zen*
Manuscript guidelines free upon request
Preferred form of initial contact: Proposal package containing short query, SASE, outline, and 3-4 sample chapters. We prefer to look at completed manuscripts as we don't contract books based on proposal.
Send submissions to—
   Eliot Stearnes, Editor
Ensure your manuscript contains proper references: footnote quotes with complete publisher data. Secure permissions for use of all copyrighted illustrations. and text.

170   Westminster John Knox Press
Subsidiary/division of Presbyterian Publishing Corp.
100 Witherspoon St, Louisville, KY 40202-1396
Phone: 502-569-5342
Fax: 502-569-5113
WWW homepage: www.pcusa.org/ppc
Director: Richard Brown
Managing Editor: Stephanie Egnotovich
Faith/denominational/cultural focus: Presbyterian, Reformed
Subject areas: Liturgy and Ritual, Prayer & Meditation, Preaching & Homiletics, Missions, Spiritual Life/Personal Religion, Religion and the Family, Ethics, Doctrinal Theology & Dogma, Process Theology, Systematic Theology, Pastoral Theology, Theological Education (methodology), Religion and Gender Studies, Psychology of Religion, Sociology of Religion, Religion and Law, Religion and Public Policy, Biblical Literature — Commentary & Hermeneutics, Biblical Literature — Cultural & Historical Contexts, Religious Education — Theory and Methodology
Types of publications: Classroom Instructional Materials, Books-on-Tape, Electronic Publications, Essay/Lecture Collections, Reprints, Devotional Guides, Liturgical Materials, Self-Help, Scholarly Monographs, General Reference, Academic Reference
Westminster John Knox publishes religious academic books in Bible, theology, ethics, worship, sociology of religion, gender studies,

pastoral theology, and homiletics, as well as general nonfiction books in all topics of religion and spirituality.

In print: 850 titles.   1997: 72 titles.

ISBN Prefix(es): 0-664

Manuscript guidelines free upon request

Preferred form of initial contact: Proposal package containing short query, outline, and sample chapters.

Send submissions to—

Academic books: Jon Berquist, Acquisitions Editor

General books: Stephanie Egnotovich, Managing Editor

171   Westview Press

Subsidiary/division of HarperCollins

5500 Central Ave, Boulder, CO 80301

Phone: 303-444-3541

Fax: 303-449-3356

WWW homepage: www.hacademic.com

Publisher: Marcus Boggs

Associate Publisher: Miriam Gilbert

Managing Editor: Janie McKenzie

Subject areas: Religious Thought/Theology, Religious Studies, Religion and Society, Sacred Literature — Commentary & Hermeneutics, Sacred Literature — Cultural & Historical Contexts

Types of publications: Essay/Lecture Collections, General Interest Nonfiction — Adult, Scholarly Monographs, Academic Reference

Westview Press is a commercial academic publisher of books intended for educated general readers, the college course market, libraries, and specialists. Its religion program offers titles by some of the most renowned religious scholars of our time, ranging from Stanley Hauerwas to David Weiss Halivni to Marcus Borg. Westview's titles cut across the range of academic inquiry into religious issues, exploring such interdisciplinary areas as religion's relationship to culture, gender, politics, science, and psychology. In addition, Westview's religion program has a global reach with works treating Buddhism, Christianity, Confucianism, Hinduism, Islam, Judaism, new religions, and other systems of belief.

Acquisitions focus for 1998-9: Texts for undergraduate courses.

In print: 40 titles.   1997: 12 titles.

3% of titles author-subsidized

ISBN Prefix(es): 0-8133

Recent/Forthcoming Titles: Stanley Hauerwas, *Wilderness Wanderings: Probing Twentieth Century Theology and Philosophy*; David Weiss Halivni, *Revelation Restored: Divine Writ and Critical Responses*; Judith Hauptman, *Rereading the Rabbis: A Woman's Voice*

Manuscript guidelines free upon request

Preferred form of initial contact: Proposal package containing outline, 2 sample chapters, letter discussing the innovativeness of the project, its intended audience and competition, and author's C.V.

Send submissions to—

Laura Parsons, Editor

172   White Cloud Press

PO Box 3400, 1190 Prospect St, Ashland, OR 97520

Phone: 541-488-6415

Fax: 541-488-6415

E-mail: sscholl@jeffnet.org

WWW homepage: www.jeffnet.org/Whitecloud

Managing Editor: Janice Lineberger

Faith/denominational/cultural focus: Interfaith

Subject areas: Comparative Religions

Types of publications: Classroom Instructional Materials, Essay/Lecture Collections, Translations, Poetry

Our basic editorial direction is to publish books that are grounded in scholarship yet accessible to a general audience. Some books, however, are more academic in orientation. We are an independent press, unaffiliated with any religious organization; the books we publish cover all the major religious traditions and new religious movements. We have special interest in mysticism, religious philosophy and translations of sacred poetry and religious texts from the great traditions.

Acquisitions focus for 1998-9: Academic-oriented comparative religion; mythology.

In print: 14 titles.   1997: 6 titles.

ISBN Prefix(es): 1-883991

No manuscript guidelines available

Preferred form of initial contact: Short written query

Limitations/Restrictions: No New Age manuscripts accepted.

173   Markus Wiener Publishers, Inc
231 Nassau Street, Princeton, NJ 08540
Ordering & Warehouse: 100 Newfield Ave, Edison, NJ 08837
Phone: 609-921-1141, 908-225-2727 (Orders/Warehouse)
Fax: 609-921-1140, 908-225-1562 (Orders/Warehouse Fax)
E-mail: wiener95@aol.com
Publisher & President: Markus Wiener
Vice President: Shelly Frisch
Editor: Susan Lorand
Administrator: Betty Reeves
Marketing: Aaron Wiener
PR, Sales: Noah Wiener
Faith/denominational/cultural focus: Judaism, Islam, Christian
Subject areas: Comparative Religions, History of Religion(s), Religion and Archaeology, Religion and Law, Talmudic Literature — Translations, Koranic Literature — Translations
Types of publications: Classroom Instructional Materials, Reprints, Translations, Scholarly Monographs, Academic Reference
Markus Wiener Publishers focus on Middle Eastern studies, history, medieval studies, world history— including the *Princeton Papers*, an interdisciplinary journal of Middle Eastern studies—and the following monograph series: "The Princeton Series on the Middle East," edited by Bernard Lewis; "Masterworks of Modern Jewish Writings"; and "Women in the Middle Ages."
Acquisitions focus for 1998-9: History of the Middle East.
In print: 30 titles.   1997: 6 titles.
ISBN Prefix(es): 0-910129, 1-55876
Recent/Forthcoming Titles: Peters, *Jihad in Classical and Modern Islam*; Heinrich Schipperges, *Hildegard of Bingen*; Will Herberg, *From Marxism to Judaism*
No manuscript guidelines available
Preferred form of initial contact: Short written query
Send submissions to—
    Susan Lorand, Editor
    Shelly Frisch, Editor

174   Wilfrid Laurier University Press
75 University Ave W, Waterloo N2A 2BS, Ontario Canada
Phone: 519-884-0710
Fax: 519-725-1399
E-mail: press@mach1.wlu.ca
WWW homepage: www.wlu.ca/~wwwpress
Subject areas: Spiritual Life/Personal Religion, Ethics, Doctrinal
    Theology & Dogma, Pluralistic/Ecumenical Theology, Comparative
    Religions, History of Religion(s), Mythology, Philosophy of Religion,
    Religion and Gender Studies, Anthropology of Religion, Religion in
    Popular Culture/Media, Religion and Law, Sacred Literature —
    Commentary & Hermeneutics, Sacred Literature — Cultural &
    Historical Contexts
Types of publications: Scholarly Monographs
Wilfrid Laurier University Press publishes scholarly books on any aspect
    of any religious tradition with series in comparative ethics; early
    Christianity and Judaism, and Women and Religion that are co-
    published with the Canadian Corporation for the Study of Religion.
In print: 47 titles.   1997: 5 titles.
Recent/Forthcoming Titles: William Arnal & Michel Desjardins, *Whose
    Historical Jesus?*; Jo-Anne Elder & Colin O'Connell, *Voices and
    Echoes: Canadian Women's Spirituality*; Renate Pratt, *In Good
    Faith: Canadian Churches Against Apartheid*
Preferred form of initial contact: Proposal package containing outline.
Send submissions to—
    Sandra Woolfrey, Director
Limitations/Restrictions: Authors must be Canadian residents.

175   Word Publishing
Subsidiary/division of Thomas Nelson Inc
PO Box 141000, Nashville, TN 37214
Phone: 800-251-4000
Fax: 615-391-5225
Publisher: Charles 'Kip' Jordan
Faith/denominational/cultural focus: Christian
Subject areas: Prayer & Meditation, Spiritual Life/Personal Religion,
    Religion and the Family, Religious Biography, Inspirational,
    Christian Living, Biblical Literature — Translations
Types of publications: Books-on-Tape, Devotional Guides, General
    Interest Nonfiction — Adult, Fiction — Adult, Academic Reference,

Hard cover Inspirational Non-Fiction, Trade Paper Inspirational
Non-Fiction

Word Publishing is a non-denominational publisher of inspirational
Christian books. The majority of our titles are hard cover volumes in
the categories of Christian living and inspiration, however we also
publish the New Century Version (NCV) translation of the Bible, the
Word Biblical Commentary Series, biographies, fiction, and more.
Our J. Countryman imprint publishes inspirational gift and specialty
products.

In print: 750 titles.   1997: 78 titles.

ISBN Prefix(es): 0-8499

Recent/Forthcoming Titles: Max Lucado, *The Great House of God*; Dr.
John MacArthur, *The MacArthur Study Bible*; Dr. Ravi Zacharias,
Cries of the Heart

No manuscript guidelines available

Preferred form of initial contact: Agented submissions only; no
unsolicited submissions accepted

176   Yale University Press

PO Box 209040, Yale Station, New Haven, CT 06220-9040

WWW homepage: www.yale.edu/yup/

Subject areas: Religious Biography, Religious Thought/Theology,
Religious Studies, Religion and Society, Sacred Literature

Types of publications: Electronic Publications (CD-ROM), Music,
Illustrated Books, Translations, Scholarly Monographs, General
Reference, Academic Reference

We publish scholarly and trade books in religious studies. Especially
strong in history, Jewish studies, Islamics, ethics, and early
Christianity.

In print: 200 titles.   1997: 15 titles.

ISBN Prefix(es): 0-300

Recent/Forthcoming Titles: Jaroslav P Pelikan, *The Illustrated Jesus
through the Centuries*; L. Duffy, *Saints and Sinners: A History of the
Popes*; B. Lang, *Sacred Games: A History of Christian Worship*

No manuscript guidelines available

Preferred form of initial contact: Short query followed by proposal
package containing SASE and outline.

Send submissions to—

Charles Grench, Editor-in-Chief

Limitations: Send query before submitting formal proposal.

177   Zondervan Publishing House

5300 Patterson Ave SE, Grand Rapids, MI 49301
Phone: 616-698-6900, 800-727-1309 (retail store customer service), 800-245-1931 (Academic Sales Specialist)
Fax: 616-698-3439, 800-934-6381 (retail store customer service)
E-mail: zpub@zph.com (main offices); jack.kragt@zph.com (Academic Sales Specialist)
WWW homepage: www.zondervan.com
Academic Sales Specialist: Jack Kragt
Academic Marketing Director: Jonathan Petersen
Faith/denominational/cultural focus: The broad evangelical spectrum.
Subject Areas: Prayer & Meditation, Vocational/Pastoral Guidance, Preaching/Homiletics, Missions, Spiritual Life/Personal Religion, Religion and the Family, Religion and Health, Religious Biography, Ethics, Doctrinal Theology/Dogma, Process Theology, Systematic Theology, Pastoral Theology, Natural Theology, Theological Education (Methodology), Comparative Religions, Sacred Languages, Philosophy of Religion, Religion and Literature, Religion and Cultural/Ethnic Studies, Psychology of Religion, Sociology of Religion, Anthropology of Religion, Religion and Archaeology, Religion and Economics, Religion and the Physical Sciences, Religion and Society, Biblical Literature — Commentary & Hermeneutics, Biblical Literature — Philology & Linguistics, Biblical Literature — Cultural/Historical Contexts, Biblical Literature — Translations, Religious Education — Elementary, Religious Education — Secondary, Religious Education — Post-secondary, Religious Education — Seminary, Religious Education — Adult
Types of Publications: Classroom Instructional Materials, Fiction — Adult, Fiction — Juvenile, Scholarly Monographs, General Reference, Academic Reference, Language Reference, Books-on-Tape, Audio-Visual, Electronic Publications (CD-ROM), Illustrated Books, Essay/Lecture Collections, Reprints, Devotional Guides, General Interest Nonfiction — Adult and Juvenile, Translations, Self-Help
Zondervan has an active program of publishing academic and reference books for biblical and theological studies and related disciplines. We are constantly in search of new works that will meet the growing needs of evangelical higher education, scholarly publication, ministry-related disciplines, as well as popular reference titles and study resources.
In print: 1,000 titles.   1997: 150 titles.

ISBN Prefix(es): 0-310

Recent/forthcoming titles: Philip Yancey, *What's So Amazing About Grace*; Billy Graham, *Just As I Am*; Kelly Monroe (ed.), *Finding God At Harvard*.

Manuscript guidelines free on request (see web site).

Preferred form of initial contact: Proposal package containing SASE, outline, sample chapters and cover letter.

Send submissions to—

Texts for classroom and individual study in biblical and theological studies, integrative studies, and issue-oriented studies:
Stan Gundry, Vice President and Editor-in-Chief

Ministry resources, Bible studies, Bible reference works (dictionaries concordances, commentaries, handbooks) for the beginning student and advanced scholar:
Jack Kuhatschek, Senior Acquisitions Editor

Resources for preachers, counselors, pastors, church planners, worship leaders, Bible teachers, elders, deacons, and ministry organizers: Jack Ruark, Senior Editor

We also review proposals that are posted through the Evangelical Christian Publishers Association's "First Edition" World Wide Web service (www.ecpa.org).

Indexes

Index 1: Faith/Denominational/Cultural Focus

Publishers are referenced by entry number

Index 2.1: Religious Life and Practice Subject Areas

Publishers are referenced by entry number

Index 2.2 Religious Thought/Theology Subject Areas

Publishers are referenced by entry number

Index 2.3: Religious Studies Subject Areas

Publishers are referenced by entry number.

Interdisciplinary Studies (*cont.*)
Harvard University Press 67
International Religious
  Foundation 75
Mercer University Press 94
Oxford University Press 104
Paragon House Publishers 107
Rudra Press 123
Swedenborg Foundation 147
**Methodologies of Study and
  Teaching**
College Press Publishing Co. 38
Faith & Life Press 55
Oxford University Press 104
University Press of Virginia 161
Mythology
Bluestar Communications 24
Bolchazy-Carducci Publishers, Inc 25
Cornell University Press 43
Crossroad Publishing Company 45
HarperSanFrancisco 66
Harvard University Press 67
Humanics Publishing Group 69
Ide House 70
Indiana University Press 71
The Johns Hopkins
  University Press 81
Oxford University Press 104
Paulist Press 110
Penn State University Press 111
Rudra Press 123
Shambhala Publications Inc 135
Snow Lion Publications, Inc 142
University of Chicago Press 154
University Press of Virginia 161
Vedanta Press 164
Samuel Weiser Inc 169
Wilfrid Laurier University Press 174
Philosophy of Religion *see also*
  Interdisciplinary Studies
Alleluia Press 8
American Bio Center 9
Ashgate Publishing Company 12
Baylor University Press 18
Bhaktivedanta Book Trust 22
Brill Academic Publishers 26
The American Institute for Patristic
  & Byzantine Studies 28
Cambridge University Press 29

College Press Publishing Co. 38
Cornell University Press 43
Crossroad Publishing Company 45
The Dordt College Press 46
Wm B Eerdmans Publishing Co 51
Foundation for *A Course
  in Miracles* 58
The Free Press 59
Genesis Publishing Co, Inc 60
HarperSanFrancisco 66
Humanics Publishing Group 69
Indiana University Press 71
InterVarsity Press 78
Mayfield Publishing 93
Oughten House Publications 103
Penn State University Press 111
Princeton University Press 115
Shambhala Publications Inc 135
M E Sharpe, Inc, Publisher 136
Snow Lion Publications, Inc 142
University of Chicago Press 154
University of Notre Dame Press 156
University of Scranton Press 157
University Press of Virginia 161
Vedanta Press 164
Wadsworth Publishing 168
Wilfrid Laurier University Press 174
Zondervan Publishing House 177
Psychology of Religion *see also*
  Interdisciplinary Studies
Baker Academic 15
Cambridge University Press 29
Crossroad Publishing Company 45
Wm B Eerdmans Publishing Co 51
Foundation for *A Course
  in Miracles* 58
The Free Press 59
Gordon Press 63
Halo Books, LLC 65
HarperSanFrancisco 66
Humanics Publishing Group 69
InterVarsity Press 78
New York University Press 100
Oughten House Publications 103
Paulist Press 110
Ragged Edge Press 117
Religious Education Press 120
Science & Behavior Books 132
Harold Shaw Publishers 137

Index 2.4: Religion and Society Subject Areas

Publishers are indexed by entry number

Index 2.5: Sacred Literature Subject Areas

Publishers are referenced by entry number

Index 2.6: Religious Education Subject Areas
Publishers are referenced by entry number

Index 3: Types of Publications

Publishers are referenced by entry number